Mark Twain

MARK TWAIN'S
Guide to Diet, Exercise, Beauty, Fashion, Investment, Romance, Health and Happiness

⚜ Words of Praise ⚜

"Nobody gets Mark Twain the way Mark Dawidziak does. Here is the master in all of his certainty, humor, and undertow. This book wonderfully underscores how contemporary Mark Twain is and always will be."

—Ken Burns, director of the film *Mark Twain* and many more award-winning documentaries

"Mark has got mighty dedicated to the restoration of Twain into our thinking and has pursued a trail of scholarship which led him to deeply research the man we so admire. We became friends early on when he covered theater and television for the *Cleveland Plain Dealer*, and have a mutual reverence and love for Mark Twain's teeming, explosive mind. This is a collection of these explosions. I think you will enjoy them. I have enjoyed them for 60 years."

—Hal Holbrook, actor

"Mark Dawidziak is as comfy and entertaining a tour guide through the world of Mark Twain as Twain himself was a tour guide through the world. In other words, *Mark Twain's Guide* is such a fun read that the only thing dry about it is the ink."

—David Bianculli, television critic and guest host for NPR's *Fresh Air*

MARK TWAIN'S
Guide  Diet, Exercise, Beauty, Fashion, Investment, Romance, Health and Happiness

Collected and Edited by
MARK DAWIDZIAK

Prospect Park Books

PROSPECT
·PARK·
BOOKS

Published by Prospect Park Books
2359 Lincoln Avenue
Altadena, CA 91001
www.prospectparkbooks.com

Distributed by Consortium Books Sales & Distribution
www.cbsd.com

Library of Congress Cataloging-in-Publication Data

Twain, Mark, 1835-1910.
 Mark Twain's guide to diet, exercise, beauty, fashion, investment, romance, health & happiness / edited by Mark Dawidziak.
   pages cm
 ISBN 978-1-938849-45-9 (hardback)
1. Twain, Mark, 1835-1910--Quotations. 2. Life--Quotations, maxims, etc. 3. Quotations, American. I. Dawidziak, Mark, 1956- editor. II. Title.
 PS1303.D345 2015
 818'.409--dc23

                        2014041276

Design & layout by David Ter-Avanesyan/Ter33Design

Printed in Canada

CONTENTS

*To Hal Holbrook, and,
many times over, he knows why*

INTRODUCTION

The Comfortable Road

The maxim assures us that confession is good for the soul (or, if you've already purchased this book, let's hope it's good for the sold). So, let's make a quick trip to the full-disclosure department. There's something wrong with the title of this book: *Mark Twain's Guide to Diet, Exercise, Beauty, Fashion, Investment, Romance, Health, and Happiness.* It's accurate, as far as it goes, but it doesn't go far enough. It's obviously too short. I realize that now. And the reader has my most humble apologies. It has been my intention from the outset to give you your money's worth, and the title is short-changing the content in this volume. Yes, there are plenty of tips on diet, exercise, beauty, fashion, investment, etc. Yet you'll also find guidance on politics, religion, parenting, and education, among other things. The advice flows freely, page after page, for as Mark Twain once observed, "Information appears to stew out of me naturally . . . The more I caulk up the sources, the more I leak wisdom."

The phrase "advice is cheap" used to mean something in this country. When the proverb was coined, after all, coins went a lot further. Advice was cheap, and you got what you paid for. Then inflation hit, and the price of advice skyrocketed. While the shopworn phrase still was treated as common currency in the marketplace of ideas, the phrase had been rendered practically meaningless, worthless, bankrupt, almost a bitter sarcasm.

Most advice you encounter these days is as worthless as ever, but it sure isn't cheap. Ever walk into a lawyer's office and ask for advice? Ever examine a bill after seeking a specialist's medical advice? Seen a therapist lately? Was it cheap?

Ever enroll in an investment seminar? It probably was a terrific get-rich plan—for the person giving the seminar. Ever feel taken after taking in one of those inspirational talks promising eternal bliss, peace, and happiness? The speaker undoubtedly left pretty happy. Ever sign up for one of those celebrity-endorsed diet plans? Chances are you were considerably lighter, all right—in the wallet.

As the dollar figure attached to advice has increased, so has the amount of it. There are countless self-help books published every year. There are infomercials coming at you from all directions on the TV landscape.

I'm not in any way suggesting that the pop-culture woods are full of charlatans. I'm not suggesting that at all. I'm saying it outright.

If all of this stuff was more than guff (that's the nice word for it), we'd be the happiest, healthiest, wealthiest, slimmest, trimmest, least-stressed, best-adjusted, best-conditioned, best-natured, most-fashionable people imaginable. Beware the type of person Mark Twain described in his story "The Man that Corrupted Hadleyburg": "He had only one vanity, he thought he could give advice better than any other person."

That person probably is a great believer in Twain's suggestion, "Nothing so needs reforming as other people's habits." This breed undoubtedly also subscribes to a saying Twain included in *Following the Equator*: "To be good is noble; but to show others how to be good is nobler and no trouble."

That's not to say there aren't honest, responsible, helpful sources of advice and inspiration. And if you've found one of those rare gems, I'd be the last to question its promises.

This book makes no such promises, but it does offer a smile or two, and perhaps some common sense in the matter of seeking and taking advice. If any of this directly leads to you being happier, that's by design. If any of this directly leads to you being healthier, that's by mistake. Fair warning on this score: Twain cautions that strict adherence to this politically incorrect advice may kill you. But then again, you may die laughing just considering his mirthful maxims and wacky witticisms.

Although laced with a delightful and offbeat brand of wisdom, Twain's advice runs contrary to almost every self-help book that has ever hit the bestseller lists. At the same time, as insane as much of this advice will seem, it brings some badly needed sanity to the discussion of advice and inspiration, diet and exercise, fashion and finance, politics and religion, parenting and childhood.

If you wish to know the spirit in which this advice is offered, consult Twain's "Seventieth Birthday" speech, delivered at Delmonico's Restaurant in Manhattan on December 5, 1905:

"I have achieved my seventy years in the usual way: by sticking strictly to a scheme of life which would kill anybody else. It sounds like an exaggeration, but that is really the common rule for attaining old age. When we examine the programme of any of these garrulous old people we always find that the habits which have preserved them would have decayed us . . . I will offer here, as a sound maxim, this: That we can't reach old age by another man's road."

The writer born Samuel Langhorne Clemens in Missouri on November 30, 1835, then gives an example of this:

"For thirty years I have taken coffee and bread at eight in the morning, and no bite nor sup until seven-thirty in the evening. Eleven hours. That is all right for me, and is wholesome, because I have never had a headache in my life, but headachy people would not reach seventy comfortably by that road, and they would be foolish to try it. And I wish to urge upon you this—which I think is wisdom—that if you find you can't make seventy by any but an uncomfortable road, don't you go.

"I desire now to repeat and emphasize that maxim: We can't reach old age by another man's road. My habits protect my life, but they would assassinate you."

There is the real grand plan for a long, happy life. And the notion of Twain's comfortable road is the path this book follows, even as it takes us through some pretty difficult territory. Cutting your own path, after all, can be as challenging as it is difficult. Sticking to it can be even trickier, particularly, as Twain warns us, there always will be someone waiting around the next turn ready to reform you, to improve you, to take all the pleasure out of your life and replace it with misery. Picture Twain standing behind this joy killer, genially puffing away on one of his beloved stogies and saying, "Don't let them do it to you . . . don't do it to yourself." Well, don't.

That's why, more than one hundred years after Mark Twain packed up his cigars and exited this realm on the back of Halley's Comet, we still turn to him for the occasional push in the right direction. "There's a Twain quote that covers this," I often find myself saying, always tempted to add, "and there's almost always a Twain quote that covers whatever is being discussed."

See, his cigars were cheap. His advice is priceless.

CHAPTER ONE

THE DESCENT.

from *The Innocents Abroad* (1869)

Exercise

Twain was quick to dismiss exercise, and any regimented kind certainly was loathsome to him. But it's not entirely true that he never took exercise. His liked to take walks, long or short, particularly if he was in the company of a cherished friend like the Reverend Joseph Hopkins Twichell, the Civil War chaplain who became pastor of Hartford's Asylum Hill Congregational Church. With Twichell along, it was as much about the talk as the walk. Twichell was his walking companion in Europe, and those walks became the basis of Twain's 1880 travel book, A Tramp Abroad. *Speaking of walks, a quote widely attributed to Mark Twain is, "Golf is a good walk spoiled." Twainiacs get downright exorcised over that one, because there's no evidence he actually said it. We'll be knocking down some of those questionable quotes as we stroll through these chapters. But he did say:*

I have never taken any exercise except sleeping and resting, and I never intend to take any. Exercise is loathsome. And it cannot be any benefit when you are tired; and I was always tired.

—1905 speech

I needed exercise, so I employed my agent in setting stranded logs and trees adrift, and I sat on a boulder and watched them go whirling and leaping head over heels down the boiling torrent. When I had had exercise enough, I made the agent take some, by running a race with one of those logs. I made a trifle by betting on the log.

—*A Tramp Abroad* (1880)

The indirect effect of the athletic atmosphere of Trinity [College, Hartford, Connecticut] is seen in the president and faculty who since the erection of the gymnasium have greatly increased in stature; the direct influence is shown by the young men themselves. The necessity of physical development needs no argument to-day and hardly an explanation. The moral effects I feel inclined to dwell upon. The time will soon come when the moral character of a man will be judged from his physical development. However, let me warn you against the danger of letting up or stopping altogether. I once had a bookkeeper who, taking up gymnastics actively, at once began to bud and blossom all over and extend in various directions; he relaxed his exertions and at length stopped his exercise, and in fourteen months lost sixteen pounds and stole $30,000. Let all take warning from this and keep up your physical development.

—1887 speech

I love work. Why, sir, when I have a piece of work to perform, I go away to myself, sit down in the shade, and muse over the coming enjoyment. Sometimes I am so industrious that I muse too long.

—quoted in *Mark Twain: A Biography* (1912)
by Albert Bigelow Paine

Get a bicycle. You will not regret it. If you live.

—"Taming the Bicycle"

It is not like studying German, where you mull along, in a groping, uncertain way, for thirty years; and at last, just as you think you've got it, they spring the subjunctive on you, and there you are. No—and I see now plainly enough, that the great pity about the German language is, that you can't fall off it and hurt yourself. There is nothing like that feature to make you attend strictly to business.

—"Taming the Bicycle"

There was a row of low stepping-stones . . . They gave me the worst falls I ever got in that street, except those which I got from dogs. I have seen it stated that no expert is quick enough to run over a dog; that a dog is always able to skip out of his way. I think that that may be true: but I think that the reason he couldn't run over the dog was because he was trying to. I did not try to run over any dog. But I ran over every dog that came along. I think it makes a great deal of difference. If you try to run over the dog he knows how to calculate, but if you are trying to miss him he does not know how to calculate, and is liable to jump the wrong way every time. It was always so in my experience. Even when I could not hit a wagon I could hit a dog that came to see me practice. They all liked to see me practice, and they all came, for there was very little going on in our neighborhood to entertain a dog.

—"Taming the Bicycle"

I had been familiar with that street for years, and had always supposed it was a dead level; but it was not, as the bicycle now informed me, to my surprise. The bicycle, in the hands of a novice . . . notices a rise where your untrained eye would not observe that one existed; it notices any decline which water will run down. I was toiling up a slight rise, but was not aware of it. It made me tug and pant and perspire; and still, labor as I might, the machine came almost to a standstill every little while. At such times the boy would say: "That's it! take a rest—there ain't no hurry. They can't hold the funeral without you."

—"Taming the Bicycle"

Well, say, this beats croquet. There's more go about it!
—quoted on football in the *New York World* (1900)

The billiard table is better than doctors—and I walk not less than ten miles every day with the cue in my hand. And the walking is not the whole of the exercise, nor the most health-giving part of it, I think. Through the multitude of the positions and attitudes it brings into play every muscle in the body and exercises them all.

—1906 letter

Now, the true charm of pedestrianism does not lie in the walking, or in the scenery, but in the talking. The walking is good to time the movement of the tongue by, and to keep the blood and the brain stirred up and active; the scenery and the woodsy smells are good to bear in upon a man an unconscious and unobtrusive charm and solace to eye and soul and sense; but the supreme pleasure comes from the talk. It is no matter whether one talks wisdom or nonsense, the case is the same, the bulk of the enjoyment lies in the wagging of the gladsome jaw and the flapping of the sympathetic ear.

—*A Tramp Abroad* (1880)

There would be a power of fun in skating if you could
do it with somebody else's muscles.

—1874 letter

I am no lazier now than I was forty years ago, but that
is because I reached the limit forty years ago. You can't
go beyond possibility.

—*Autobiography*

CHAPTER TWO

DRINKING SLUMGULLION.

from *Roughing It* (1872)

Diet

The bill of fare in this chapter is a smorgasbord of advice on dietary matters. Much food for thought here, including Twain's thoughts on such childhood favorites as Southern corn bread and the watermelon. His food philosophy was captured in the quote, "Part of the secret of success in life is to eat what you like and let the food fight it out inside." Are you swallowing that? So if you've been left thoroughly confused by all those diet plans and all that conflicting medical advice (where do coffee, carbs, and chocolate stand this month?), chew this over:

In the matter of diet—which is another main thing—I have been persistently strict in sticking to the things which didn't agree with me until one or the other of us got the best of it. But last spring I stopped frolicking with mince pie after midnight; up to then I had always believed it wasn't loaded.

—1905 speech

Sagebrush is a very fair fuel, but as a vegetable it is a distinguished failure. Nothing can abide the taste of it but the jackass and his illegitimate child the mule.

—*Roughing It* (1872)

Yes, Agassiz does recommend authors to eat fish, because the phosphorus in it makes brain. So far you are correct. But I cannot help you to a decision about the amount you need to eat—at least not with certainty. If the specimen composition you send is about your fair usual average, I suggest that perhaps a couple of whales would be all you would want for the present. Not the largest kind, but simply good middling-sized whales.

—"Answers to Correspondents" in
Sketches New and Old (1875)

But when the time comes that a man has had his dinner, then the true man comes to the surface.

—1902 speech

Only strangers eat tamarinds—but they only eat them once.

—*Roughing It* (1872)

On the continent, you can't get a rare beefsteak—everything is as overdone as a martyr.

—1897 notebook entry

Then he poured for us a beverage which he called "Slumgullion," and it is hard to think he was not inspired when he named it. It really pretended to be tea, but there was too much dish-rag, and sand, and old bacon-rind in it to deceive the intelligent traveler.

—*Roughing It* (1872)

You can get what the European hotel-keeper thinks is coffee, but it resembles the real thing as hypocrisy resembles holiness.

—*A Tramp Abroad* (1880)

Recipe for German Coffee. Take a barrel of water and bring it to a boil; rub a chiccory berry against a coffee berry, then convey the former into the water. Continue the boiling and evaporation until the intensity of the flavor and aroma of the coffee and chiccory has been diminished to a proper degree; then set aside to cool.

—*A Tramp Abroad* (1880)

After a few months' acquaintance with European "coffee," one's mind weakens, and his faith with it, and he begins to wonder if the rich beverage of home, with its clotted layer of yellow cream on top of it, is not a mere dream, after all, and a thing which never existed.

—*A Tramp Abroad* (1880)

Foreigners cannot enjoy our food, I suppose, any more than we can enjoy theirs. It is not strange; for tastes are made, not born. I might glorify my bill of fare until I was tired; but after all, the Scotchman would shake his head, and say, "Where's your haggis?" and the Fijan would sigh and say, "Where's your missionary?"

—*A Tramp Abroad* (1880)

Then there is the beefsteak. They have it in Europe, but they don't know how to cook it. Neither will they cut it right . . . Imagine a poor exile contemplating that inert thing; and imagine an angel suddenly sweeping down out of a better land and setting before him a mighty porterhouse steak an inch and a half thick, hot and sputtering from the griddle; dusted with fragrant pepper; enriched with little melting bits of butter of the most unimpeachable freshness and genuineness; the precious juices of the meat trickling out and joining the gravy, archipelagoed with mushrooms . . . could words describe the gratitude of this exile?

—*A Tramp Abroad* (1880)

I have been entertaining a stranger; I have been at it two days and two nights, and am worn, and jaded, and in fact defeated . . . He is classified in natural history as the Long Clam . . . If you don't know him personally, leave him alone; take him at hearsay and meddle no further. He is a bivalve . . . You swallow the Long Clam—and history begins.

—1889 speech

We picked up one excellent word—a word worth traveling to New Orleans to get; a nice limber, expressive,
handy word—"lagniappe." They pronounce it lan-
ny-yap. It is Spanish—so they said. We discovered it at
the head of a column of odds and ends in the Picayune,
the first day; heard twenty people use it the second;
inquired what it meant the third; adopted it and got
facility in swinging it the fourth. It has a restricted
meaning . . . It is the equivalent of the thirteenth
roll in a "baker's dozen." It is something thrown in,
gratis, for good measure. The custom originated in
the Spanish quarter of the city . . . If the waiter in the
restaurant stumbles and spills a gill of coffee down the
back of your neck, he says, "For lagniappe, sah," and
gets you another cup without extra charge.

—*Life on the Mississippi* (1883)

In the summer the table was set in the middle of that
shady and breezy floor, and the sumptuous meals—well,
it makes me cry to think of them. Fried chicken, roast
pig; wild and tame turkeys, ducks, and geese; venison
just killed; squirrels, rabbits, pheasants, partridges,

prairie-chickens; biscuits, hot batter cakes, hot buckwheat cakes, hot "wheat bread," hot rolls, hot corn pone; fresh corn boiled on the ear, succotash, butter-beans, string-beans, tomatoes, peas, Irish potatoes, sweet potatoes; buttermilk, sweet milk, "clabber"; watermelons, muskmelons, cantaloupes—all fresh from the garden; apple pie, peach pie, pumpkin pie, apple dumplings, peach cobbler—I can't remember the rest.

—*Autobiography*

The way that the things were cooked was perhaps the main splendor—particularly a certain few of the dishes. For instance, the corn bread, the hot biscuits and wheat bread, and the fried chicken. These things have never been properly cooked in the North—in fact, no one there is able to learn the art, so far as my experience goes. The North thinks it knows how to make corn bread, but this is mere superstition. Perhaps no bread in the world is quite so good as Southern corn bread, and perhaps no bread in the world is quite so bad as the Northern imitation of it.

—*Autobiography*

The North seldom tries to fry chicken, and this is well; the art cannot be learned north of the line of Mason and Dixon, nor anywhere in Europe. This is not hearsay; it is experience that is speaking. In Europe it is imagined that the custom of serving various kinds of bread blazing hot is "American," but that is too broad a spread; it is custom in the South, but is much less than that in the North.

—*Autobiography*

I spent some part of every year at the farm until I was twelve or thirteen years old . . . I know how the wild blackberries looked, and how they tasted, and the same with the pawpaws, the hazelnuts, and the persimmons . . . I know the taste of maple sap, and when to gather it, and how to arrange the troughs and the delivery tubes, and how to boil down the juice, and how to hook the sugar after it is made, also how much better hooked sugar tastes than any that is honestly come by, let bigots say what they will.

—*Autobiography*

I know how a frozen apple looks, in a barrel down cellar
in the wintertime, and how hard it is to bite, and how
the frost makes the teeth ache, and yet how good it
is, notwithstanding . . . I know the look of an apple
that is roasting and sizzling on a hearth on a winter's
evening, and I know the comfort that comes of eating
it hot, along with some sugar and a drench of cream.

—*Autobiography*

I know the delicate art and mystery of so cracking
hickory nuts and walnuts on a flatiron with a hammer
that the kernels will be delivered whole, and I know
how the nuts, taken in conjunction with winter apples,
cider, and doughnuts, make old people's old tales and
old jokes sound fresh and crisp and enchanting.

—*Autobiography*

I know the look of green apples and peaches and pears
on the trees, and I know how entertaining they are
when they are inside of a person.

—*Autobiography*

To a Christian who has toiled months and months
in Washoe . . . and the broken spirit of the contrite
heart finds joy and peace only in Limburger cheese
and lager beer—unto such a Christian, verily the
Occidental Hotel is Heaven on the half shell . . .
Here you are expected to breakfast on salmon, fried
oysters, and other substantials from 6 till half-past
12; you are required to lunch on cold fowl and so
forth, from half-past 12 until 3; you are obliged to
skirmish through a dinner comprising such edibles
as the world produces, and keep it up, from 3 until
half-past 7; you are then compelled to lay siege to the
tea-table from half-past 7 until 9 o'clock, at which
hour, if you refuse to move upon the supper works
and destroy oysters gotten up in all kinds of seductive
styles until 12 o'clock, the landlord will certainly be
offended, and you might as well move your trunk to
some other establishment. [It is a pleasure to me to
observe, incidentally, that I am on good terms with
the landlord yet.]

—*Territorial Enterprise*, 1864

I know how a prize watermelon looks when it is sunning its fat rotundity among pumpkin vines and "simblins"; I know how to tell when it is ripe without "plugging" it; I know how inviting it looks when it is cooling itself in a tub of water under the bed, waiting; I know how it looks when it lies on the table in the sheltered great floor space between house and kitchen, and the children gathered for the sacrifice and their mouths watering; I know the crackling sound it makes when the carving knife enters its end . . . I can see its halves fall apart and display the rich red meat and the black seeds . . . a luxury fit for the elect; I know how a boy looks behind a yard-long slice of that melon, and I know how he feels; for I have been there.

—*Autobiography*

I know the taste of the watermelon which has been honestly come by, and I know the taste of the watermelon which has been acquired by art. Both taste good, but the experienced know which tastes best.

—*Autobiography*

The true Southern watermelon is a boon apart, and not to be mentioned with commoner things. It is chief of this world's luxuries, king by the grace of God over all the fruits of the earth. When one has tasted it, he knows what the angels eat. It was not a Southern watermelon that Eve took; we know it because she repented.

—*Pudd'nhead Wilson* (1894)

It's about the first time I ever stole a watermelon. "Stole" is a strong word. Stole? Stole? No, I don't mean that. It was the first time I ever withdrew a watermelon. It was the first time I ever extracted a watermelon . . . I extracted that watermelon from a farmer's wagon while he was inside negotiating with another customer. I carried that watermelon to one of the secluded recesses of the lumber-yard, and there I broke it open. It was a green watermelon. Well, do you know when I saw that I began to feel sorry—sorry—sorry. It seemed to me that I had done wrong . . . I think I was just eleven . . . I knew what a boy ought to do who extracted a watermelon like that . . . So I gathered up the biggest fragments, and I carried them back to the farmer's wagon, and I restored the watermelon—what was left of it. And I made him give me a good one in place of it, too. And I told him he ought be ashamed of himself going around working off worthless, old, green watermelons on trusting purchasers who had to rely on him . . . And if he didn't reform, I told him I'd see that he didn't get any more of my trade . . . You know that man was as contrite as a revivalist's last convert . . . And he drove off a better man.

—1906 speech

A full belly is little worth where the mind is starved, and the heart.

—*The Prince and the Pauper* (1881)

CHAPTER THREE

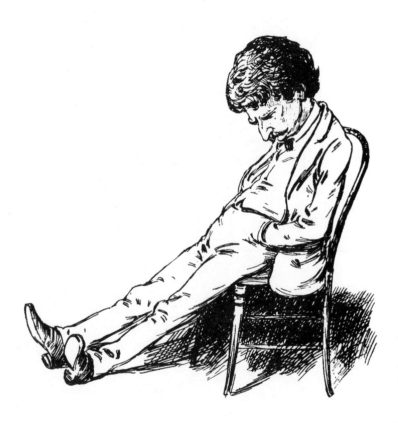

from *Life* magazine (August 9, 1883)

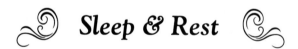 **Sleep & Rest**

Mark Twain described himself as "a naturally lazy man." He was a master at avoiding work, and, therefore, a strong advocate of rest and relaxation. "I have seen slower, quieter, more listless, lazier people than I am, but they were dead." Could you ask for a more astute guide into the land of nod? Nod once, if you're not asleep.

Well enough for old folks to rise early, because they have done so many mean things all their lives they can't sleep anyhow.

—*Mark Twain's Notebook* (1935)

Rise early. It is the early bird that catches the worm. Don't be fooled by this absurd saw; I once knew a man who tried it. He got up at sunrise and a horse bit him.

—*Mark Twain's Notebook* (1935)

Wisdom teaches us that none but birds should go out early, and that not even birds should do it unless they are out of worms.

—"New Year's Day" (1866)

Go to bed early, get up early—this is wise. Some authorities say get up with one thing, some with another. But a lark is really the best thing to get up with. It gives you a splendid reputation with everybody to know that you get up with the lark; and if you get the right kind of a lark, and work at him right, you can easily train him to get up at half-past nine, every time—it is no trick at all.

—1882 speech

In America, we hurry—which is well; but when the day's work is done, we go on thinking of losses and gains, we plan for the morrow, we even carry our business cares to bed with us, and toss and worry over them when we ought to be restoring our racked bodies and brains with sleep.

—*The Innocents Abroad* (1869)

In our dreams—I know it!—we do make the journeys we seem to make: we do see the things we seem to see; the people, the homes, the cats, the dogs, the birds, the whales, are real, not chimeras; they are living spirits, not shadows; and they are immortal and indestructible. They go whither they will; they visit all resorts, all points of interest, even the twinkling suns that wander in the wastes of space. That is where those strange mountains are which slide from under our feet while we walk, and where those vast caverns are whose bewildering avenues close behind us and in front when we are lost, and shut us in. We know this because there are no such things here, and they must be there, because there is no other place.

—"My Platonic Sweetheart"

My dream-artist can draw anything, and do it perfectly;
he can paint with all the color and all the shades,
and do it with delicacy and truth; he can place before
me vivid images of palaces, cities, hamlets, hovels,
mountains, valleys, lakes, skies, glowing in sunlight or
moonlight, or veiled in driving gusts of snow or rain,
and he can set before me people who are intensely
alive, and who feel, and express their feelings in their
faces, and who also talk and laugh, sing and swear.
And when I wake I can shut my eyes and bring back
those people, and the scenery and the buildings; and
not only in general view, but often in nice detail. . . .

—"My Platonic Sweetheart"

Many ships have good beds, but no ship has very good
ones. In the matter of beds all ships have been badly
edited, ignorantly edited, from the beginning. The
selections of beds is given to some hearty, strong-backed,
self-made man, when it ought to be given to a frail
woman accustomed from girlhood to backaches and
insomnia. Nothing is so rare, on either side of the ocean,

as a perfect bed . . . In Noah's Ark the beds were simply scandalous. Noah set the fashion, and will endure in one degree of modification or another till the next flood.

—*Following the Equator* (1897)

We did not mind the noise, being tired, but, doubtless, the reader is aware that it is almost an impossible thing to go to sleep when you know that people are looking at you.

—*The Innocents Abroad* (1869)

But Jim was asleep. Tom looked kind of ashamed, because you know a person always feels bad when he is talking uncommon fine and thinks the other person is admiring, and that other person goes to sleep that way. Of course he oughtn't to go to sleep, because it's shabby; but the finer a person talks the certainer it is to make you sleep, and so when you come to look at it it ain't nobody's fault in particular; both of them's to blame.

—*Tom Sawyer Abroad* (1894)

I hate a man who goes to sleep at once; there is a sort of indefinable something about it which is not exactly an insult, and yet is an insolence; and one which is hard to bear, too.

—*A Tramp Abroad* (1880)

I lay there fretting over this injury, and trying to go to sleep; but the harder I tried, the wider awake I grew. I got to feeling very lonely in the dark, with no company but an undigested dinner. My mind got a start by and by, and began to consider the beginning of every subject which has ever been thought of; but it never went further than the beginning; it was touch and go; it fled from topic to topic with a frantic speed. At the end of an hour my head was in a perfect whirl and I was dead tired.

—*A Tramp Abroad* (1880)

[I] turned in and slept like a log—I don't mean a brisk, fresh, green log, but an old dead, soggy rotten one, that never turns over or gives a yelp.

—1871 letter

To stretch out and go to sleep, even on stony and frozen ground, after pushing a wagon and two horses fifty miles, is a delight so supreme that for the moment it almost seems cheap at the price.

—*Roughing It* (1872)

The boat came ashore for us, and in a little while the clouds and the rain were all gone. The moon was beaming tranquilly down on land and sea, and we two were stretched upon the deck sleeping the refreshing sleep and dreaming the happy dreams that are only vouchsafed to the weary and the innocent.

—*Roughing It* (1872)

Since forty I have been regular about going to bed and getting up—and that is one of the main things. I have made it a rule to go to bed when there wasn't anybody left to sit up with; and I have made it a rule to get up when I had to.

—1905 speech

In due time we spread our blankets in the warm sand between two large boulders and soon fell asleep, careless of the procession of ants that passed in through rents in our clothing and explored our persons. Nothing could disturb the sleep that fettered us, for it had been fairly earned, and if our consciences had any sins on them they had to adjourn court for that night, anyway.

—*Roughing It* (1872)

The following might just as easily slip into Chapter Five's discussion of alcohol, but one of the writer's closest friends, author and editor William Dean Howells, left behind this memory of Mark Twain's bedtime battles:

In those days he was troubled with sleeplessness, or, rather, with reluctant sleepiness, and he had various specifics for promoting it. At first it had been champagne just before going to bed, and we provided that, but later he appeared from Boston with four bottles of lager-beer under his arms; lager-beer, he said now, was the only thing to make you go to sleep, and we provided that. Still later, on a visit I paid him at Hartford, I learned that hot Scotch was the only soporific worth considering, and Scotch whiskey duly found its place on our sideboard. One day, very long afterward, I asked him if he were still taking hot Scotch to make him sleep. He said he was not taking anything. For a while he had found going to bed on the bath-room floor a soporific; then one night he went to rest in his own bed at ten o'clock, and had gone promptly to sleep without anything. He had done the like with the like effect ever since. Of course, it amused him; there were few experiences of life, grave or gay, which did not amuse him, even when they wronged him.

CHAPTER FOUR

SOLID COMFORT

from *Adventures of Huckleberry Finn* (1885)

Smoking

Cigars were Mark Twain's lifelong companions. No other writer is more associated with the stogie, the cheroot, the seegar, the call-it-what-you-will. Twain once said that he came into this world asking for a light and that he expected to go out of it blowing smoke rings. Although not exactly the poster boy for the Surgeon General's office, Twain passed his cigar, like a baton for an all-American relay team, to such later humorists as H.L. Mencken and Groucho Marx. It was a favorite prop for the wittily inclined, and we're not just blowing smoke here. Twain probably never said, "To cease smoking is the easiest thing. I ought to know. I've done it a thousand times." It's another one of those quotes without verification or citation, but it undoubtedly sums up his attitude toward what his friend Rudyard Kipling called "the cheery light Of stumps burned to Friendship and Pleasure and Work and Fight."

First . . . don't smoke—that is, don't smoke to excess.
I am seventy-three and a half years old, and have been
smoking for seventy-three of them. But I never smoke
to excess—that is, I smoke in moderation, only one
cigar at a time.

—"Advice to Girls" speech (1909)

Now whenever I buy a cigar that costs six cents I am
suspicious of it. When it costs four and a quarter or
five cents I smoke it with confidence.

—*Autobiography*

As an example to others, and not that I care for moderation myself, it has always been my rule never to
smoke when asleep, and never refrain when awake.
It is a good rule.

—1905 speech

As the darkness closed down and the stars came out
and spangled the great mirror with jewels, we smoked
meditatively in the solemn hush and forgot our troubles and our pains.

—*Roughing It* (1872)

When I was a youth I used to take all kinds of pledges, and do my best to keep them, but I never could, because I didn't strike at the root of the habit—the desire; I generally broke down within the month. Once I tried limiting a habit. That worked tolerably well for a while. I pledged myself to smoke but one cigar a day. I kept the cigar waiting until bedtime, then I had a luxurious time with it. But desire persecuted me every day and all day long; so, within the week I found myself hunting for larger cigars than I had been used to smoke; then larger ones still, and still larger ones. Within the fortnight I was getting cigars made for me—on a yet larger pattern. They still grew and grew in size. Within the month my cigar had grown to such proportions that I could have used it as a crutch. It now seemed to me that a one-cigar limit was no real protection to a person, so I knocked my pledge on the head and resumed my liberty.

—*Following the Equator* (1897)

I have made it a rule never to smoke more than one cigar at a time. I have no other restrictions.

—1905 speech

I allow myself the fullest possible marvel of inspiration, consequently, I smoke fifteen cigars during my five hours' working labor, and if my interest reaches the enthusiastic point, I smoke more. I smoke with all my might, and allow no intervals.

—1882 letter

Why, my boy, when they use to tell me I would shorten my life ten years by smoking they little knew the devotee they were wasting their puerile words upon—they little knew how trivial and valueless I would regard a decade that had no smoking in it!

—1870 letter

I smoke in bed until have to go to sleep; I wake up in the night, sometimes once, and I never waste any of these opportunities to smoke. The habit is so old and dear and precious to me that I would feel as you, sir, would feel if you should lose the only moral you've got. . . if you've got one; I am making no charges.

—1905 speech

I said to a friend, "I want to know if you can direct me to an honest tobacco merchant who will tell what is the worst cigar in the New York market . . . I want real tobacco. If you will do this and I find this man is as good as his word, I will guarantee him a regular market for a fair amount of his cigars."

We found a tobacco dealer who would tell the truth . . . He produced what he called the very worst cigars he had in his shop. He let me experiment with one then and there. The test was satisfactory.

This was, after all, the real thing . . . I discovered that the "worst cigars," so called, are the best for me, after all.

—*Mark Twain's Speeches* (1910)

I will grant, here, that I have stopped smoking now and then, for a few months at a time, but it was not on principle, it was only to show off; it was to pulverize those critics who said I was a slave to my habits and couldn't break my bonds.

—1905 speech

CHAPTER FIVE

FIRST SUPPER IN FRANCE.

from *The Innocents Abroad* (1869)

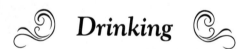 **Drinking**

We left coffee, tea, and other such beverages where they belong: in the chapter set aside for diet. Here we take up the more spirited topic of drink with a bit more authority to it. Twain's favorite liquor was Scotch, and his favorite way to consume said Scotch was his beloved hot Scotch. The ingredients? Coming right up:

Livy, my darling, I want you to be sure and remember to have, in the bathroom when I arrive, a bottle of Scotch whiskey, a lemon, some crushed sugar, and a bottle of Angostura bitters. Ever since I have been in London I have taken in a wine glass what is called a cock-tail (made with those ingredients) before breakfast, before dinner, and just before going to bed.

—1874 letter to his wife

Dear St. Andrew, The whisky arrived in due course from over the water; last week one bottle of it was extracted from the wood and inserted into me, on the installment plan, with this result: that I believe it to be the best, smoothest whiskey now on the planet. Thanks, oh, thanks: I have discarded Peruna.

Hoping that you three are well and happy and will be coming back before the winter sets in.

I am, Sincerely Yours, Mark.

—1906 letter to Andrew Carnegie,
thanking him for sending a case of Scotch

I gave him a pipe and a chair and made him welcome. I also comforted him with a hot Scotch whiskey; gave him another one; then still another—hoping always for his story. After a fourth persuader, he drifted into it himself, in a quite simple and natural way.

—*A Connecticut Yankee in King Arthur's Court* (1889)

Scotch whiskey . . . I always take it at night as a preventative of toothache. I have never had the toothache; and what is more, I never intend to have it.

—*Europe and Elsewhere* (1923)

Statistics—statistics—why statistics are more precious and useful than any other one thing in this world, except whiskey—I mean hymnbooks.

—1880 speech

When I was two years of age she asked me not to drink, and then I made a resolution of total abstinence. That I have adhered to it and enjoyed the beneficent effects of it through all time, I owe to my grandmother. I have never drunk a drop from that day to this of any kind of water.

—*Sketches New and Old* (1875)

What marriage is to morality, a properly conducted licensed liquor traffic is to sobriety.

—1895 notebook entry

Laffan gave me two bottles of whiskey and a box of cigars—I go to sea nobly equipped.

—1893 letter to William Dean Howells

Give an Irishman lager for a month, and he's a dead man. An Irishman is lined with copper, and the beer corrodes it. But whiskey polishes the copper and is the saving of him.

—*Life on the Mississippi* (1883)

John Wagner, the oldest man in Buffalo—one hundred and four years old . . . . and yet has never tasted a drop of liquor in his life—unless—unless you count whiskey.

—*Sketches New and Old* (1875)

I love a drink, but I never encouraged drunkenness by harping on its alleged funny side.

—quoted in *Abroad with Mark Twain and Eugene Field* (1922)

Doctor Rice's friend . . . came home drunk and explained it to his wife, and his wife said to him, "John, when you have drunk all the whiskey you want, you ought to ask for sarsaparilla." He said, "Yes, but when I have drunk all the whiskey I want I can't say sarsaparilla."

—1902 speech

Then everybody traveled by steamboat, everybody drank, and everybody treated everybody else. "Now most everybody goes by railroad, and the rest don't drink." In the old times the barkeeper owned the bar himself, "and was gay and smarty and talky and all jeweled up, and was the toniest aristocrat on the boat; used to make $2,000 on a trip. A father who left his son a steamboat bar, left him a fortune. Now he leaves him board and lodging; yes, and washing, if a shirt a trip will do. Yes, indeedy, times are changed. Why, do you know, on the principal line of boats on the Upper Mississippi, they don't have any bar at all! Sounds like poetry, but it's the petrified truth.

—*Life on the Mississippi* (1883)

There was an attractive spot among the trees where were a great many wooden tables and benches; and there one could sit in the shade and pretend to sip at his foamy beaker of beer while he inspected the crowd. I say pretend, because I only pretended to sip, without really sipping. That is the polite way; but when you are ready to go, you empty the beaker at a draught.

—*A Tramp Abroad* (1880)

We bought a bottle or so of beer here; at any rate they called it beer, but I knew by the price that it was dissolved jewelry, and I perceived by the taste that dissolved jewelry is not good stuff to drink.

—*A Tramp Abroad* (1880)

How solemn and beautiful is the thought that the earliest pioneer of civilization, the van-leader of civilization, is never the steamboat, never the railroad, never the newspaper, never the Sabbath-school, never the missionary—but always whiskey!

—*Life on the Mississippi* (1883)

The system of refusing the mere act of drinking and leaving the desire in full force, is unintelligent war tactics, it seems to me.

—*Following the Equator* (1897)

Never refuse to do a kindness unless the act would work great injury to yourself, and never refuse to take a drink—under any circumstances.

—*Mark Twain's Notebook* (1935)

As for drinking, I have no rule about that. When the others drink I like to help.

—"Seventieth Birthday" speech (1905)

CHAPTER SIX

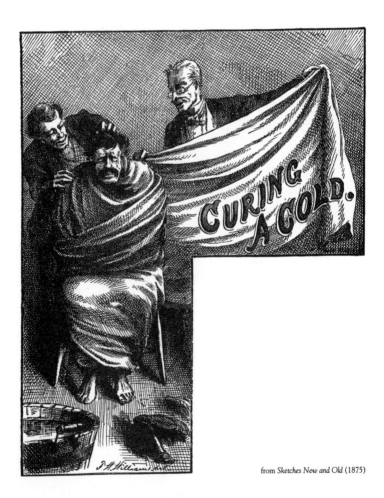

from *Sketches New and Old* (1875)

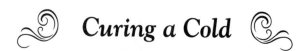 **Curing a Cold**

There's nothing like being ill to make you sick . . . of doctors, medicine, and, of course, the most notorious of all symptoms: free advice from an army of interns practicing without a license.

The Autocrat of Russia possesses more power than any other man in the earth; but he cannot stop a sneeze.

—*Following the Equator* (1897)

Tom lay thinking. Presently it occurred to him that he wished he was sick; then he could stay home from school. Here was a vague possibility. He canvassed his system. No ailment was found, and he investigated again. This time he thought he could detect colicky symptoms, and he began to encourage them with considerable hope.

—*The Adventures of Tom Sawyer* (1876)

One should not bring sympathy to a sick man. It is always kindly meant, and of course it has to be taken— but it isn't much of an improvement on castor oil. One who has a sick man's true interest at heart will forbear spoken sympathy, and bring him surreptitious soup and fried oysters and other trifles that the doctor has tabooed.

—Letter to friend and early
mentor Mary Mason Fairbanks

As far as being on the verge of being a sick man I don't take any stock in that. I have been on the verge of being an angel all of my life, but it's never happened yet.

> —quoted in *Mark Twain: A Biography* (1912)
> by Albert Bigelow Paine

Medicine has its office, it does its share and does it well; but without hope back of it, its forces are crippled and only the physician's verdict can create that hope when the facts refuse to create it.

> —Letter to Dr. W.W. Baldwin (1903 or '04)

Any mummery will cure, if the patient's faith is strong in it.

> —*A Connecticut Yankee in King Arthur's Court* (1889)

Man seems to be a rickety poor sort of a thing, any way you take him; a kind of British Museum of infirmities and inferiorities. He is always undergoing repairs. A machine that was as unreliable as he is would have no market.

> —"The Lowest Animal" (1896)

Man starts in as a child and lives on diseases to the end as a regular diet.

> —quoted in *Mark Twain: A Biography* (1912)
> by Albert Bigelow Paine

Most cursed of all are the dentists who made too many parenthetical remarks—dentists who secure your instant and breathless interest in a tooth by taking a grip on it, and then stand there and drawl through a tedious anecdote before they give the dreaded jerk. Parentheses in literature and dentistry are in bad taste.

> —*A Tramp Abroad* (1880)

The physicians think they are moved by regard for the best interest of the public. Isn't there a little touch of self-interest back of it all? It seems to me there, and I don't claim to have all the virtues—only nine or ten of them.

> —1901 speech

All dentists talk while they work. They have inherited this from their professional ancestors, the barbers.

> —*Europe and Elsewhere* (1923)

The Emperor commanded the physicians of greatest renown to appear before him for consultation . . . were they proper healers or merely assassins? Then the principal assassin, who was also the oldest doctor in the land and the most venerable in appearance, answered and said . . . "Sometimes they seem to help nature a little—a very little—but, as a rule, they merely do damage."

—"Two Little Tales" (1901)

Whose property is my body? Probably mine. I so regard it. If I experiment with it, who must be answerable? I, not the State. If I choose injudiciously, does the State die? Oh, no.

—1901 speech

Dear Sir (or Madam):—I try every remedy sent to me. I am now on No. 67. Yours is 2,653. I am looking forward to its beneficial results.

—quoted in *My Father, Mark Twain* (1931)
by Clara Clemens

The first time I began to sneeze, a friend told me to go and bathe my feet in hot water and go to bed. I did so. Shortly afterward, another friend advised me to get up and take a cold shower-bath. I did that also. Within the hour, another friend assured me that it was policy to "feed a cold and starve a fever." I had both. So I thought it best to fill myself up for the cold, and then keep dark and let the fever starve awhile . . .

I started down toward the office, and on the way encountered another bosom friend, who told me that a quart of salt-water, taken warm, would come as near curing a cold as anything in the world. I hardly thought I had room for it, but I tried it anyhow. The result was surprising. I believed I had thrown up my immortal soul . . . If I had another cold in the head, and there were no course left me but to take either an earthquake or a quart of warm saltwater, I would take my chances on the earthquake . . . I came across a lady who had just arrived from over the plains, and who said she had lived in a part of the country where doctors were scarce, and had from necessity acquired considerable skill in the treatment of simple "family complaints." I knew she must have had much experience, for she appeared to be a hundred and fifty years old.

She mixed a decoction composed of molasses, aquafortis, turpentine, and various other drugs, and instructed me to take a wine-glass full of it every fifteen minutes. I never took but one dose; that was enough; it robbed me of all moral principle, and awoke every unworthy impulse of my nature.

I finally concluded to visit San Francisco, and the first day I got there a lady at the hotel told me to drink a quart of whiskey every twenty-four hours, and a friend up-town recommended precisely the same course. Each advised me to take a quart; that made half a gallon. I did it, and still live.

Now, with the kindest motives in the world, I offer for the consideration of consumptive patients the variegated course of treatment I have lately gone through. Let them try it; if it don't cure, it can't more than kill them.

—*Sketches New and Old* (1875)

Since I was seven years old I have seldom taken a dose of medicine, and have still seldomer needed one. But up to seven I lived exclusively on allopathic medicines. Not that I needed them, for I don't think I did; it was for economy; my father took a drug store for a debt, and it made cod-liver cheaper than the other breakfast foods. We had nine barrels of it, and it lasted me seven years. Then I was weaned. The rest of the family had to get along with rhubarb and ipecac and such things, because I was the pet. I was the first Standard Oil trust. By the time the drug store was exhausted my health was established and there has never been much the matter with me since.

—1905 speech

By some happy fortune I was not seasick. That was a thing to be proud of. I had not always escaped before. If there is one thing in the world that will make a man peculiarly and insufferably self-conceited, it is to have his stomach behave itself, the first day at sea, when nearly all his comrades are seasick.

—*The Innocents Abroad* (1869)

I was always told that I was a sickly and precarious and tiresome and uncertain child, and lived mainly on allopathic medicines during the first seven years of my life. I asked my mother about this, in her old age—she was in her eighty-eighth year—and said:

"I suppose that during all that time you were uneasy about me?"

"Yes, the whole time."

"Afraid I wouldn't live?"

After a reflective pause—ostensibly to think out the facts—"No—afraid you would."

—*Autobiography*

Do not undervalue the headache. While at its sharpest it seems a bad investment; but when relief begins, the unexpired remainder is worth four dollars a minute.

—*Following the Equator* (1897)

The only way to keep your health is to eat what you don't want, drink what you don't like, and do what you'd druther not.

—*Following the Equator* (1897)

I can quit any of nineteen injurious habits at any time, and without discomfort or inconvenience . . . after a few hours the desire is discouraged and comes no more. Once I tried my scheme in a large medical way. I had been confined to my bed several days with lumbago. My case refused to improve. Finally the doctor said: "My remedies have no fair chance. Consider what they have to fight, besides the lumbago. You smoke extravagantly, don't you?'

"Yes."

"You take coffee immoderately?"

"Yes."

"You eat all kinds of things that are dissatisfied with each other's company?"

"Yes."

"You drink two hot Scotches every night?"

"Yes."

"Very well, there you can see what I have to contend with. We can't make any progress the way the matter stands. You must make a reduction in these things."

"I can't, doctor."

"Why can't you?"

"I lack the will-power. I can cut them off entirely, but I can't moderate them."

He said that would answer . . . I cut off all those things for two days and two nights . . . and at the end of forty-eight hours the lumbago was discouraged and left me. I was a well man; so I gave thanks and took to these delicacies again.

It seemed a valuable medical course, and I recommended it to a lady. She had run down and down and down, and had at last reached a point where medicines no longer had any helpful effect upon her. I said I knew I could put her upon her feet in a week. It brightened her up . . . So I said she must stop swearing and drinking and smoking and eating for four days, and then she would be all right again . . . but she said she could not stop swearing and smoking and drinking, because she had never done these things. So there it was. She had neglected her habits . . . She was a sinking vessel, with no freight to throw overboard . . . Why, even one or two little bad habits could have saved her, but she was just a moral pauper.

—*Following the Equator* (1897)

There was a good deal of cholera around the Mississippi Valley in those days, and my mother used to dose us children with a medicine called Patterson's Patent Pain Killer. She had an idea that cholera was worse than the medicine, but then she had never taken any of the stuff. It went down our insides like liquid fire and fairly doubled us up.

—1908 story for children in Hamilton, Bermuda

In 1844 Kneipp filled the world with the wonder of the water cure. Mother wanted to try it, but on sober second thought she put me through. A bucket of ice water was poured over to see the effect. Then I was rubbed with flannels, a sheet was dipped in the water, and I was put to bed. I perspired so much that mother put a life preserver to bed with me . . . three times. When a boy, mother's new methods got me so near death's door she had to call in the family physician to pull me out.

—1901 speech

I was the subject of my mother's experiment. She was wise. She made experiments cautiously. She didn't pick out just any child in the flock. No, she chose judiciously. She chose one she could spare, and she couldn't spare the others. I was the choice child of the flock, so I had to take all of the experiments.

—1901 speech

[The measles]: It brought me within a shade of death's door. It brought me to where I no longer felt any interest in anything, but, on the contrary, felt a total absence of interest—which was most placid and tranquil and sweet and delightful and enchanting. I have never enjoyed anything in my life any more than I enjoyed dying that time . . . The word had been passed and the family notified to assemble around the bed and see me off . . . They were all crying, but that did not affect me. I took but the vaguest interest in it and that merely because I was the center of all this emotional attention and was gratified by it and vain of it.

—*Autobiography*

CHAPTER SEVEN

from *Sketches New and Old* (1875)

Stress Management

Blowing off steam

There is no evidence that Mark Twain was familiar with the word lalochezia, coined in the late nineteenth century by a French physician. But there's a hell of a good chance he would have approved of it in the strongest possible terms. Lalochezia is the emotional relief an individual feels from using profane language. And Mark Twain was a firm believer in the power of swearing to reduce and release stress. When Twain let his temper fly, the air around him was dense with cigar smoke and blue words.

In certain trying circumstances, urgent circumstances, desperate circumstances, profanity furnishes a relief denied even to prayer.

> —quoted in *Mark Twain: A Biography* (1912)
> by Albert Bigelow Paine

Profanity is more necessary to me than is immunity from colds.

> —1877 letter

The spirit of wrath—not the words—is the sin; and the spirit of wrath is cursing. We begin to swear before we can talk.

> —*Following the Equator* (1897)

For it is not the word that is the sin, it is the spirit back of the word. When an irritated lady says "oh!" the spirit back of it is "damn!" and that is the way it is going to be recorded against her. It always makes me so sorry when I hear a lady swear like that. But if she says "damn," and says it in an amiable, nice way, it isn't going to be recorded at all.

> —1906 speech

The idea that no gentleman ever swears is all wrong. He can swear and still be a gentleman if he does it in a nice and benevolent and affectionate way.

—1906 speech

He began with that word "H . . ." That's a long word and a profane word. I don't remember what the word was now, but I recognized the power of it. I had never used that language myself, but at that moment I was converted. It has been a great refuge for me in time of trouble. If a man doesn't know that language he can't express himself on strenuous occasions. When you have that word at your command, let trouble come.

—1908 speech

"Pass the bread, you son of a skunk!" No, I forget—skunk was not the word; it seems to me it was still stronger than that; I know it was, in fact, but it is gone from my memory, apparently. However, it is no matter—probably it was too strong for print, anyway. It is the landmark in my memory which tells me where I first encountered the vigorous new vernacular of the occidental plains and mountains.   —*Roughing It* (1872)

[A] quadrilateral, astronomical, incandescent son-of-a-bitch.

—1903 letter

And the next second after that I was astraddle of the main limb and blaspheming my luck in a way that made my breath smell of brimstone.

—*Roughing It* (1872)

If I cannot swear in heaven I shall not stay there.

—1898 notebook entry

There ought to be room in this house to swear in. It's dangerous to have to suppress an emotion like that.

—quoted in *Mark Twain: A Biography* (1912)
by Albert Bigelow Paine

There is one thing very sure—I can't keep my temper in New York. The cars and carriages always come along and get in the way just as I want to cross a street, and if there is any thing that can make a man soar into flights of sublimity in the matter of profanity, it is that thing.

—1867 letter to Alta California (San Francisco)

Let us swear while we may, for in Heaven it will not be allowed.

> —1898 notebook entry

When it comes down to pure ornamental cursing, the native American is gifted above the sons of men.

> —*Roughing It* (1872)

You do not swear anymore now, of course, because you can't find any words that are long enough or strong enough to fit the case. You feel degraded and ignominious and subjugated. And there and then you say that you will go away from New York and start over again; and that you will never come back to settle permanently till you have learned to swear with the utmost fluency in seventeen different languages.

> —1867 letter to Alta California (San Francisco)

It fairly curdled my blood to hear him swear with such awful swears. I never had my blood curdled before, so I put some in a bottle to look at it.

> —*Stars and Stripes*, 1870

By and by, when I came to, I sent down to the rum mill on the corner and hired an artist by the week to sit up nights and curse that stranger, and give me a lift occasionally in the daytime when I came to a hard place.

—*Sketches New and Old* (1875)

This was a red rag to the bull. He raged and stormed so (he was crossing the river at the time) that I judged it made him blind, because he ran over the steering-oar of a trading-scow. Of course the traders sent up a volley of red-hot profanity. Never was a man so grateful as Mr. Bixby was; because he was brimful, and here were subjects who could talk back. He threw open a window, thrust his head out, and such an irruption followed as I never had heard before. The fainter and farther away the scowmen's curses drifted, the higher Mr. Bixby lifted his voice and the weightier his adjectives grew. When he closed the window he was empty. You could have drawn a seine through his system and not caught curses enough to disturb your mother with.

—*Life on the Mississippi* (1883)

You never heard such accomplished profanity . . . I
never enjoyed profanity as I enjoyed it then—more
than if I had been uttering it myself. There is nothing
like listening to an artist—all his passions passing away
in lava, smoke, thunder, lightning, and earthquake.

—1905 speech

He swore at me artfully . . . the air was fairly blue with
oaths . . . He must have had the Devil's dictionary at
his tongue's end.

—*Stars and Stripes*, 1870

All through the first ten years of my married life I
kept a constant and discreet watch upon my tongue
while in the house, and went outside and to a distance
when circumstances were too much for me and I was
obliged to seek relief. I prized my wife's respect and
approval above all the rest of the human race's respect
and approval. I dreaded the day when she should dis-
cover that I was but a whited sepulcher partly freighted
with suppressed language. I was so careful, during ten
years, that I had not a doubt that my suppressions had
been successful. Therefore I was quite as happy in my

guilt as I could have been if I had been innocent. . .

But at last an accident exposed me. I went into the bathroom one morning to make my toilet, and carelessly left the door two or three inches ajar. It was the first time that I had ever failed to take the precaution of closing it tightly. I knew the necessity of being particular about this, because shaving was always a trying ordeal for me, and I could seldom carry it through to a finish without verbal helps. Now this time I was unprotected, and did not suspect it . . . My temper jumped up several degrees in a moment and my remarks rose accordingly, both in loudness and vigor of expression. But I was not troubled, for the bathroom door was a solid one and I supposed it was firmly closed . . . Then I straightened up, gathered my reserves, and let myself go like a cavalry charge. In the midst of that great assault, my eye fell upon that gaping door, and I was paralyzed . . . I saw that young and beautiful face; and I saw the gracious eyes with a something in them which I had never seen there before. They were snapping and flashing with indignation. I felt myself crumbling; I felt myself shrinking away to nothing under that accusing gaze. I stood silent under that desolating fire for as much as a minute, I should say—it seemed a very, very long time. Then my wife's lips parted, and from them issued my latest bathroom remark. The language perfect, but the expression unpractical, apprentice-like, ignorant, inexperienced, comically inadequate, absurdly weak and unsuited to the great language. In my lifetime I had never heard anything so out of tune, so inharmonious, so incongruous, so ill suited to each other as were those mighty words set to that feeble music. I tried to keep from laughing, for I was a guilty person in deep need of charity and mercy. I tried to keep from bursting, and I succeeded—until she gravely said, "There, now you know how it sounds."

Oh, then I exploded! I said, "Oh, Livy, if it sounds like that, God forgive me, I will never do it again."

Then she had to laugh, herself. Both of us broke into convulsions, and went on laughing until we were exhausted.

—*Autobiography*

CHAPTER EIGHT

THE DUKE WENT FOR HIM.

from *Adventures of Huckleberry Finn* (1885)

Anger Management

Writing about her famous father, thirteen-year-old Susy Clemens observed, "He has got a temper, but we all of us have in this family." Friends and family remembered Twain's anger as something magnificent to behold. Memories of such outbursts often scorched his conscience, but attempts to reform on this front were about as successful as efforts to give up drinking and swearing. There was no way to completely tame the Twain. His Vesuvian anger could be incited by inanimate objects or a long-held grudge . . . or the wording of a book contract. Don't we all have those triggers, as different as they might be? Here's how Twain tried to deal with them:

If a person offend you and you are in doubt as to whether it was intentional or not, do not resort to extreme measures. Simply watch your chance and hit him with a brick.

—1882 speech

It takes me a long time to lose my temper, but once lost I could not find it with a dog.

—1894 notebook entry

When angry, count four; when very angry, swear.

—*Pudd'nhead Wilson* (1894)

My anger grew to a frenzy. I finally did what all persons before me have done, clear back to Adam—resolved to throw something.

—*A Tramp Abroad* (1880)

A letter written in a passion is a mistake . . . It usually wrongs two persons, and *always* wrongs one—yourself.

—quoted in *Mark Twain: A Biography* (1912)
by Albert Bigelow Paine

Your native warm temper suddenly jumped to the front, and for the moment its influence was more powerful than your mother's, and abolished it. In that instance you were eager to flash out a hot rebuke and enjoy it. You did enjoy it, didn't you?

—*What Is Man?* (1906)

When you get an exasperating letter what happens? If you are young, you answer it promptly, instantly—and mail the thing you have written. At forty what do you do? By that time you have found out that a letter written in passion is a mistake in ninety-nine cases out of a hundred.

—quoted in *Mark Twain: A Biography* (1912)
by Albert Bigelow Paine

You never saw a bigoted, opinionated, stubborn, narrow-minded, self-conceited almighty man in your life but he had stuck in one place ever since he was born and thought God made the world and dyspepsia and bile for his especial comfort and satisfaction.

—1868 speech

He [a publisher] has been dead a quarter of a century now. My bitterness against him has faded away and disappeared. I feel only compassion for him and if I could send him a fan I would.

—*Mark Twain in Eruption* (1940)

Complexities annoy me; then irritate me; then this progressive feeling presently warms into anger. I cannot get far in the reading of the commonest and simplest contract—with its "parties of the first part," and "parties of the second part," and "parties of the third part"—my temper is all gone.

—*Autobiography*

My days are given up to cursings—both loud and deep—for I am reading the *Huckleberry Finn* proofs. They don't make a very great many mistakes, but those that do occur are of a nature to make a man curse his teeth loose.

—1884 letter to William Dean Howells

To this day I lose my balance and send an overwarm letter . . . two or three times a year. But that is better than doing it a hundred times a year, as I used to do years ago. Perhaps I write as many as ever, but I pigeonhole them. They ought not to be thrown away. Such a letter a year or so old is as good as a sermon to the man who wrote it. It makes him feel small and shabby.

—quoted in *Mark Twain: A Biography* (1912)
by Albert Bigelow Paine

The proof-reading on the P&P [*The Prince and the Pauper*] cost me the last rags of my religion.

—1884 letter to William Dean Howells

CHAPTER NINE

WORTH A MILLION.

from *Roughing It* (1872)

Maintaining a Positive Outlook

If lives are measured by how much joy they bring into the world, Twain, despite his outbursts and his dark ruminations on "the damned human race," more than lives up to his towering reputation. Use this chapter as a handy source for spirit-lifting.

Do not part with your illusions. When they are gone, you may still exist, but you have ceased to live.

—*Following the Equator* (1897)

Happiness is a Swedish sunset—it is there for all, but most of us look the other way and lose it.

—1899 notebook entry

Grief can take care of itself; but to get the full value of joy you must have somebody to divide it with.

—*Following the Equator* (1897)

The best way to cheer yourself up is to try to cheer somebody else up.

—*Mark Twain's Notebook* (1935)

Good friends, good books, and a sleepy conscience: this is the ideal life.

—*Mark Twain's Notebook* (1935)

I always feel young when I come in the presence of young people.

—1905 speech

A good and wholesome thing is a little harmless fun in this world; it tones a body up and keeps him human and prevents him from souring.

—*Personal Recollections of Joan of Arc* (1896)

By trying we can easily learn to endure adversity— another man's I mean.

—*Following the Equator* (1897)

The perfection of wisdom, and the end of true philosophy, is to proportion our wants to our possessions, our ambitions to our capacities, we will then be a happy and a virtuous people.

—"The Enemy Conquered; or, Love Triumphant"

For your race, in its poverty, has unquestionably one really effective weapon—laughter . . . against the assault of laughter nothing can stand.

—*The Mysterious Stranger* (1916)

Humor is mankind's greatest blessing.

—quoted in *Mark Twain: A Biography* (1912) by Albert Bigelow Paine

A healthy and wholesome cheerfulness is not necessarily impossible to any occupation.

—*Sketches New and Old* (1875)

Happiness ain't a thing in itself—it's only a contrast with something that ain't pleasant.

—"Captain Stormfield's Visit to Heaven"

You can't depend on your judgment when your imagination is out of focus.

—*Mark Twain's Notebook* (1935)

What is a government without energy? And what is a man without energy? Nothing—nothing at all. What is the grandest thing in *Paradise Lost*—the Arch-Fiend's terrible energy! What was the greatest feature in Napoleon's character? His unconquerable energy! Sum all the gifts that man is endowed with, and we give our greatest share of admiration to his energy. And today, if I were a heathen, I would rear a statue to Energy and fall down and worship it!

—1860 letter

Humor is the great thing, the saving thing after all. The minute it crops up, all our hardnesses yield, all our irritations and resentments flit away, and a sunny spirit takes their place.

—"What Paul Bourget Thinks of Us"

There are three things which come to my mind which I consider excellent advice: First . . . don't smoke—that is, don't smoke to excess . . . Second, don't drink—that is, don't drink to excess. Third, don't marry—I mean, to excess.

—1909 speech

Do something every day that you don't want to do; this is the golden rule for acquiring the habit of doing your duty without pain.

—*Following the Equator* (1897)

We can secure other people's approval if we do right and try hard; but our own is worth a hundred of it, and no way has been found out of securing that.

—*Following the Equator* (1897)

"Don't you worry, and don't you hurry." I know that phrase by heart, and if all other music should perish out of the world it would still sing to me.

—1900 speech

Good breeding consists in concealing how much we think of ourselves and how little we think of the other person.

—1898 notebook entry

Let us be thankful for the fools; but for them the rest of us could not succeed.

—*Following the Equator* (1897)

Few things are harder to put up with than the annoyance of a good example.

—*Pudd'nhead Wilson* (1894)

Drag your thoughts away from your troubles—by the ears, by the heels, or any other way, so you can manage it; it's the healthiest thing a body can do.

—*The American Claimant* (1899)

When you are expecting the worst, you get something that is not so bad, after all.

—*A Connecticut Yankee in King Arthur's Court* (1889)

Work and play are words used to describe the same thing under different conditions.

—quoted in *More Maxims of Mark*
(1927, edited by M. Johnson)

Work consists of whatever a body is obliged to do. Play consists of whatever a body is not obliged to do.

—*The Adventures of Tom Sawyer* (1876)

It is a blessed provision of nature that at times like these, as soon as a man's mercury has got down to a certain point there comes a revulsion, and he rallies. Hope springs up, and cheerfulness along with it, and then he is in good shape to do something for himself, if anything can be done.

—*A Connecticut Yankee in King Arthur's Court* (1889)

No, Sir, not a day's work in all my life. What I have done I have done because it has been play. If it had been work I shouldn't have done it. Who was it who said, "Blessed is the man who has found his work"? Whoever it was he had the right idea in his mind. Mark you, he says his work, not somebody else's work. The work that is really a man's own work is play and not work at all. Cursed is the man who has found some other man's work and cannot lose it."

—*New York Times* interview, 1905

An occasional compliment is necessary to keep up one's self-respect. The plan of the newspaper is good and wise; when you can't get a compliment any other way, pay yourself one.

—1894 notebook entry

In the matter of courage we all have our limits. There never was a hero who did not have his bounds . . . I know a man who is not afraid to sleep with a rattlesnake, but you could not get him to sleep with a safety-razor.

—"Courage"

Courage is resistance to fear, mastery of fear—not absence of fear. Except a creature be part coward it is not a compliment to say it is brave; it is merely a loose misapplication of the word.

—*Pudd'nhead Wilson* (1894)

It has never been my way to bother much about things which you can't cure.

—*A Connecticut Yankee in King Arthur's Court* (1889)

Cheer up, the worst is yet to come.

—1894 letter

CHAPTER TEN

IT'S THE FASHION.

from *A Tramp Abroad* (1880)

Beauty Tips

Here is another Twain "quote" for which there is no verification: "Twenty-four years ago I was strangely handsome; in San Francisco in the rainy season I was often mistaken for fair weather." That one falls into the category of, if he didn't say it, he should have. Or, to accurately quote director John Ford's The Man Who Shot Liberty Valance, "When the legend becomes fact, print the legend." Fair weather or ill, Twain had some gorgeous advice on the subject of beauty.

In true beauty, more depends upon right location and judicious distribution of feature than upon multiplicity of them. The very combination of colors which in a volcanic eruption would add beauty to a landscape might detach it from a girl.

—*The American Claimant* (1892)

One frequently only finds out how really beautiful a really beautiful woman is after considerable acquaintance with her; and the rule applies to Niagara Falls, to majestic mountains, and to mosques—especially to mosques.

—*The Innocents Abroad* (1869)

One is apt to overestimate beauty when it is rare.

—*The Innocents Abroad* (1869)

There are women who have an indefinable charm in their faces which makes them beautiful to their intimates, but a cold stranger who tried to reason the matter out and find this beauty would fail.

—*A Tramp Abroad* (1880)

She had a beautiful complexion when she first came, but it faded out by degrees in an unaccountable way. However, it is not lost for good. I found the most of it on my shoulder afterwards.

—*Sketches New and Old* (1875)

All things change except barbers, the ways of barbers, and the surroundings of barbers. These never change.

—*Sketches New and Old* (1875)

A barber seldom rubs you like a Christian.

—*Sketches New and Old* (1875)

When red-headed people are above a certain social grade their hair is auburn.

—*A Connecticut Yankee in King Arthur's Court* (1889)

Forty years ago I was not so good-looking. A looking glass then lasted me three months. Now I can wear it out in two days.

—*Autobiography*

CHAPTER ELEVEN

"I'LL PAY YOU IN PARIS."

from *The Innocents Abroad* (1869)

Fashion

The fashion item most associated with Mark Twain unquestionably was his trademark white suit. There are pictures of Twain in a white suit before 1906, but it was at age seventy-one that he began wearing them in public—all the time. He called it his "dontcareadam suit." And he knew he was making a fashion statement. With flowing white hair, he knew this was an attention grabber. "It is human nature to take delight in exciting admiration," he said. "It is what prompts children to say 'smart' things, and do absurd ones, and in other ways 'show off' when company is present." He was not above showing off.

Clothes make the man. Naked people have little or no influence in society.

—quoted in *More Maxims of Mark* (1927)

Modesty died when clothes were born.

—quoted in *Mark Twain: A Biography* (1912)
by Albert Bigelow Paine

Their costumes, as to architecture, were the latest fashion intensified; they were rainbow-hued; they were hung with jewels—chiefly diamonds. It would have been plain to any eye that it had cost something to upholster these women.

—*The Gilded Age* (1873)

"You haven't seen a person with clothes on. Oh, well, you haven't lost anything."

—visiting angel in *Letters from the Earth* (1962)

Some civilized women would lose half their charm without dress, and some would lose all of it.

—"Woman, God Bless Her!" speech (1882)

No woman can look as well out of fashion as in it.

—quoted in *Mark Twain's
Travels with Mr. Brown* (1940)

Strip the human race, absolutely naked, and it would be a real democracy. But the introduction of even a rag of tiger skin, or a cowtail, could make a badge of distinction and be the beginning of a monarchy.

—*Mark Twain's Notebook* (1935)

Whatever a man's age, he can reduce it several years by putting a bright-colored flower in his button-hole.

—*The American Claimant* (1899)

We must put up with our clothes as they are—they have their reason for existing. They are on us to expose us—to advertise what we wear them to conceal. They are a sign; a sign of insincerity; a sign of suppressed vanity; a pretense that we desire gorgeous colors and form; and we put them on to propagate that lie and back it up.

—*Following the Equator* (1897)

Never run after your own hat—others will be delighted
to do it. Why spoil their fun?

> —quoted in *Abroad with Mark Twain and*
> *Eugene Field* (1922)

I was at a luncheon party, and Archdeacon Wilberforce
was there also . . . I did steal his hat, but he began by
taking mine . . . He came out before the luncheon
was over, and sorted the hats in the hall, and selected
one which suited. It happened to be mine . . . There
were results that were pleasing to me—possibly to him.
He found out whose hat it was, and wrote me saying
it was pleasant that all the way home, whenever he
met anybody his gravities, his solemnities, his deep
thoughts, his eloquent remarks were all snatched
up by the people he met, and mistaken for brilliant
humorisms.

I had another experience. It was not unpleasing.
I was received with a deference which was entirely
foreign to my experience . . . so that before I got home
I had a much higher opinion of myself than I have ever
had before or since.

> —1907 speech

The most fashionably dressed lady was Mrs. G.C. She wore a pink satin dress, plain in front but with a good deal of rake to it—to the train, I mean; it was said to be two or three yards long. One could see it creeping along the floor some little time after the woman was gone.

—*Sketches New and Old* (1875)

A policeman in plain clothes is a man; in his uniform he is ten. Clothes and title are the most potent thing, the most formidable influence, in the earth. They move the human race to willing and spontaneous respect for the judge, the general, the admiral, the bishop, the ambassador, the frivolous earl, the idiot duke, the sultan, the king, the emperor. No great title is efficient without clothes to support it.

—"The Czar's Soliloquy"

Be careless in your dress if you must, but keep a tidy soul.

—*Following the Equator* (1897)

As for me, give me comfort first, and style afterwards.

—*A Connecticut Yankee in King Arthur's Court* (1889)

We have to send soldiers—we can't get out of that—
but we can disguise them. It is the way England does
in South Africa. Even Mr. Chamberlain himself takes
pride in England's honorable uniform, and makes the
army down there wear an ugly and odious and appro-
priate disguise, of yellow stuff such as quarantine flags
are made of, and which are hoisted to warn the healthy
away from unclean disease and repulsive death. This
cloth is called khaki. We could adopt it. It is light,
comfortable, grotesque, and deceives the enemy, for
he cannot conceive of a soldier being concealed in it.

—"To the Person Sitting in Darkness"

What sorry shows and shadows we are. Without our
clothes and our pedestals we are poor things and
much of a size; our dignities are not real, our pomps
are shams. At our best and stateliest we are not suns, as
we pretended, and teach, and believe, but only candles;
and any bummer can blow us out.

—"The Memorable Assassination"

And now for the white suit:

> I talked in a snow-white fulldress, swallow-tail and all,
> and dined in the same. It's a delightful impudence. I
> think I will call it my dontcareadam suit. But in the
> case of the private dinner I will always ask permission
> to wear it first saying: "Dear Madam, may I come in
> my dontcareadams?"

> —quoted in *My Father, Mark Twain* (1931
> by Clara Clemens

When I find myself in assemblies like this, with everybody in black clothes, I know I possess something that
is superior to everybody else's . . . You don't know
whether they are clean or not, because you can't see
. . . If you wear white clothes, you are clean . . . I am
proud to say I can wear a white suit of clothes without a blemish for three days. If you need any further
instruction in the matter of clothes I shall be glad to
give it to you . . . I do not want to boast. I only want
to make you understand that you are not clean.

—1907 speech

This suit, I may say, is the uniform of the Ancient and Honorable Order of Purity and Perfection, of which organization I am president, secretary, treasurer, and sole member. I may add that I don't know of any one else who is eligible. You see, when a man gets to be 71, as I am, the world begins to look somber and dark. I believe we should do all we can to brighten things up and make ourselves look cheerful. You can't do that by wearing black, funereal clothes. And why shouldn't a man wear white? It betokens purity and innocence. I'm in favor of peek-a-boo waists and décolleté costumes. The most beautiful costume is the human skin, but since it isn't conventional or polite to appear in public in that garb alone, I believe in wearing white. I don't know anything more hideous or disgusting in men's attire than the black clawhammer coat. A group of men thus adorned remind me more of a flock of crows than anything else. About the most becoming get up I ever saw in my life was out in the Sandwich Islands thirty years ago, where a native who wanted to appear at his best usually appeared in a pair of eyeglasses.

—quoted in the *Chicago Daily Tribune* (1906)

I have found that when a man reaches the advanced age of 71 years as I have, the continual sight of dark clothing is likely to have a depressing effect upon him. Light-colored clothing is more pleasing to the eye and enlivens the spirit. Now, of course, I cannot compel every one to wear such clothing just for my especial benefit, so I do the next best thing and wear it myself.

—quoted in *The New York Times* (1906)

As for black clothes, my aversion to them is incurable.

—1909 letter

CHAPTER TWELVE

THE DELEGATE'S INTERESTING GAME.

from *The Gilded Age* (1873)

Finance
&
Investment

One of the most frequently quoted Twain lines on money matters is this gem: "A banker is a fellow who lends you his umbrella when the sun is shining and wants it back the minute it begins to rain." It certainly captures the spirit of Twain's thoughts on bankers, but it's yet another line that comes up bankrupt in the attribution account. We can't prove he didn't say it, of course, but we have verification sound as a dollar bill for these:

There are two times in a man's life when he should not speculate: when he can't afford it, and when he can.

—*Following the Equator* (1897)

All you need in life is ignorance and confidence, and then Success is sure.

—1887 notebook entry

There is an old-time toast which is golden for its beauty. "When you ascend the hill of prosperity, may you not meet a friend."

—*Following the Equator* (1897)

Prosperity is the best protector of principle.

—*Following the Equator* (1897)

Few of us can stand prosperity. Another man's, I mean.

—*Following the Equator* (1897)

He says that the primary rule of business success is loyalty to your employer. That's all right—as a theory. What is the matter with loyalty to yourself?

—1901 speech

Honesty is the best policy—when there is money in it.

—1901 speech

Let your sympathies and your compassion be always with the underdog in the fight—this is magnanimity; but bet on the other one—this is business.

—quoted in *Mark Twain: A Biography* (1912)
by Albert Bigelow Paine

I find that, as a rule, when a thing is a wonder to us it is not because of what we see in it, but because of what others have seen in it. We get almost all our wonders at second hand . . . By and by you sober down, and then you perceive that you have been drunk on the smell of somebody else's cork.

—*Following the Equator* (1897)

The lack of money is the root of all evil.

—quoted in *More Maxims of Mark* (1927)

Let us not be too particular. It is better to have old, second hand diamonds than none at all.

—*Following the Equator* (1897)

I consider that a broker goes according to the instincts that are in him, and means no harm, and fulfills his mission according to his lights, and has a right to live, and be happy in a general way, and be protected by the law to some extent, just the same as a better man. I consider that brokers come into the world with souls—I am satisfied they do; and if they wear them out in the course of a long career of stock-jobbing, have they not a right to come in at the eleventh hour and get themselves half-soled, like old boots, and be saved at last? Certainly—the father of the tribe did that, and do we say anything against Barabbas for it to-day? No! we concede his right to do it; we admire his mature judgment in selling out of a worked-out mine of iniquity and investing in righteousness, and no man denies, or even doubts, the validity of the transaction. Other people may think as they please, and I suppose I am entitled to the same privilege; therefore, notwithstanding what others may believe, I am of the opinion that a broker can be saved. Mind, I do not say that a broker *will* be saved, or even that is uncommon likely that such a thing will happen—I only say that Lazarus was raised from the dead, the five thousand were fed with twelve loaves of bread, the water was turned into wine, the Israelites crossed the Red Sea dry-shod, and a broker *can* be saved. True, the angel that accomplishes the task may require all eternity to rest himself in, but has that got anything to do with the establishment of the proposition? Does it invalidate it? Does it detract from it? I think not.

—"Daniel in the Lion's Den—And
Out Again All Right" (1864)

Beautiful credit! The foundation of modern society. Who shall say that this is not the golden age of mutual trust, of unlimited reliance upon human promises? That is a peculiar condition of society which enables a whole nation to instantly recognize point and meaning in the familiar newspaper anecdote, which puts into the mouth of a distinguished speculator in lands and mines this remark: "I wasn't worth a cent two years ago, and now I owe two millions of dollars."

—*The Gilded Age* (1873)

OCTOBER: This is one of the peculiarly dangerous months to speculate in stocks. The others are July, January, September, April, November, May, March, June, December, August, and February.

—*Pudd'nhead Wilson* (1894)

He is now fast rising from affluence to poverty.

—"Rev. Henry Ward Beecher's Farm"

For all the talk you hear about knowledge being such a wonderful thing, instinct is worth forty of it for real unerringness.

—*Tom Sawyer Abroad* (1894)

The offspring of riches: Pride, vanity, ostentation, arrogance, tyranny.

—quoted in *Mark Twain: A Biography* (1912)
by Albert Bigelow Paine

Even Noah got no salary for the first six months—partly on account of the weather and partly because he was learning navigation.

—*Mark Twain in Eruption* (1940)

Some men worship rank, some worship heroes, some worship power, some worship God, & over these ideals they dispute & cannot unite—but they all worship money.

—*Mark Twain's Notebook* (1935)

The less a man knows the bigger the noise he makes and the higher the salary he commands.

—"How I Edited an Agricultural Paper"

I was seldom able to see an opportunity until it had ceased to be one.

—*Autobiography*

I never count any prospective chickens when I know that Providence knows where the nest is.

—1883 letter

My axiom is, to succeed in business, avoid my example.

—1901 speech

Tell the truth or trump—but get the trick.

—*Pudd'nhead Wilson* (1894)

The lust of gain—a lust which does not stop short of the penitentiary or the jail to accomplish its ends.

—1901 speech

Behold the fool saith, "Put not all thine eggs in the one basket"—which is but a manner of saying, "Scatter your money and your attention"; but the wise man saith, "Put all your eggs in the one basket and— WATCH THAT BASKET."

—*Pudd'nhead Wilson* (1894)

Money-lust has always existed, but not in the history of the world was it ever a craze, a madness, until your time and mine.

—1905 letter

Like all other nations, we worship money and the possessors of it—they being our aristocracy, and we have to have one. We like to read about rich people in the papers; the papers know it, and they do their best to keep this appetite liberally fed.

—*Autobiography*

It isn't the sum you get, it's how much you can buy with it, that's the important thing; and it's that that tells whether your wages are high in fact or only high in name.

—*A Connecticut Yankee in King Arthur's Court* (1889)

The timid man yearns for full value and demands a tenth. The bold man strikes for double value and compromises on par.

—*Following the Equator* (1897)

It is sound judgment to put on a bold face and ply your hand for a hundred times what it worth; forty-nine times out of fifty nobody dares to "call," and you roll in the chips.

—*A Connecticut Yankee in King Arthur's Court* (1889)

A dollar picked up in the road is more satisfaction to you than the ninety-and-nine which you had to work for, and money won at faro or in stock snuggles into your heart in the same way.

—"The Shrine of St. Wagner"

Stocks went on rising; speculations went mad; bankers, merchants, lawyers, doctors, mechanics, laborers, even the very washerwomen and servant-girls, were putting up their earnings on silver stocks, and every sun that rose in the morning went down on paupers enriched and rich men beggared. What a gambling carnival it was! . . . And then—all of a sudden, out went the bottom and everything and everybody went to ruin and destruction! The wreck was complete. The bubble scarcely left a microscopic moisture behind it. I was an early beggar and a thorough one. My hoarded stock were not worth the paper they were printed on . . . I felt meaner and lowlier, and more despicable than the worms.

—*Roughing It* (1872)

The poor are always good to each other. When a man with millions gives a hundred thousand dollars it makes a great noise in the world, but he does not miss it. It's noise in the wrong place; it's the widow's mite that makes no noise but does the best work.

—1901 speech

One must keep one's character. Earn a character first if you can, and if you can't, then assume one. From the code of morals I have been following and revising and revising for 72 years I remember one detail. All my life I have been honest—comparatively honest. I could never use money I had not made honestly—I could only lend it.

—1907 speech

CHAPTER THIRTEEN

THE LECTURER'S AUDIENCE.

from *A Tramp Abroad* (1880)

Experience

&

Education

All right, class, settle down. You're all going to enjoy the guest lecturer for today. A good deal of what he has to say on this subject can be applied to your previous lessons. Sit up straight. Take notes. Life will quiz you on this:

We all do no end of feeling, and we mistake it for thinking.

—"Corn-pone Opinions"

The most permanent lessons in morals are those which come, not of booky teaching, but of experience.

—*A Tramp Abroad* (1880)

But as to this matter of education, the first thing that strikes you is how much teaching has really been done and how much is worthless cramming.

—1887 speech

The mere knowledge of a fact is pale; but when you come to *realize* your fact, it takes on color. It is all the difference between hearing of a man being stabbed to the heart, and seeing it done.

—*A Connecticut Yankee in King Arthur's Court* (1889)

It is best to prove things by experiment; then you *know*; whereas if you depend on guessing and supposing and conjecturing, you will never get educated.

—*Eve's Diary* (1905)

What you needed, I reckon, was less book-learning and more bread-and-butter learning.

—*The American Claimant* (1892)

It is from experiences such as mine that we get our education of life. We string them into jewels or into tinware, as we may choose.

—quoted in *Mark Twain: A Biography* (1912)
by Albert Bigelow Paine

If you are going to find out the facts of a thing, what's the sense in guessing out what ain't the facts and wasting ammunition?

—*Tom Sawyer, Detective* (1896)

Supposing is good, but finding out is better.

—*Mark Twain in Eruption* (1940)

How empty is theory in the presence of fact!

—*A Connecticut Yankee in King Arthur's Court* (1889)

Opinions based upon theory, superstition, and ignorance are not very precious.

—1900 letter

Experience, the only logic sure to convince a diseased imagination and restore it to rugged health.

—*The American Claimant* (1892)

If there wasn't anything to find out, it would be dull. Even trying to find out and not finding out is just as interesting as trying to find out and finding out; and I don't know but more so.

—*Eve's Diary* (1905)

War talk by men who have been in a war is always interesting; whereas, moon talk by a poet who has not been in the moon is likely to be dull.

—*Life on the Mississippi* (1883)

We should be careful to get out of an experience only the wisdom that is in it—and stop there; lest we be like the cat that sits down on a hot stove-lid. She will never sit down on a hot stove-lid again—and that is well; but also she will never sit down on a cold one anymore.

—*Following the Equator* (1897)

Learnin' by expe'ence . . . There's lot of such things, and *they* educate a person . . . Uncle Abner said that the person that had took a bull by the tail once had learnt sixty or seventy times as much as a person that hadn't, and said a person that started in to carry a cat home by the tail was gitting knowledge that was always going to be useful to him, and warn't ever going to grow dim or doubtful.

—*Tom Sawyer Abroad* (1894)

Experience teaches us only one thing at a time—and hardly that, in my case.

—1893 letter

I was gratified to be able to answer promptly, and I did. I said I didn't know.

—*Life on the Mississippi* (1883)

But we are all that way: when we know a thing we have only scorn for other people who don't happen to know it.

—*Personal Recollections of Joan of Arc* (1896)

Plain question and plain answer make the shortest
road out of most perplexities.

—*Life on the Mississippi* (1883)

Learning softeneth the heart and breedeth gentleness
and charity.

—*The Prince and the Pauper* (1881)

A man who can't learn stands in his own light.

—"An Entertaining Article"

Training is everything. The peach was once a bitter
almond; cauliflower is nothing but cabbage with a
college education.

—*Pudd'nhead Wilson* (1894)

There's many a way to win in this world, but none of
them is worth much, without good hard work back of it.

—*Personal Recollections of Joan of Arc* (1896)

Inestimably valuable is training, influence, education,
in right directions.

—*What Is Man?* (1906)

Training—training is everything; training is all there is to a person.

—*A Connecticut Yankee in King Arthur's Court* (1889)

This was good training, persistent training; and in all arts it is training that brings the act to perfection.

—*Christian Science* (1907)

Training is potent. Training toward higher and higher, and ever higher ideals is worth any man's thought and labor and diligence.

—*What Is Man?* (1906)

From the cradle to the grave, during all his waking hours, the human being is under training.

—*What Is Man?* (1906)

There is a large improvement, then, in two years? . . . You see there *is* use in training. Keep on. Keep faithfully on. You are doing well.

—*What Is Man?* (1906)

My lord, the power of training! Of influence! Of education!

—*A Connecticut Yankee in King Arthur's Court* (1889)

Training does wonderful things . . . There is nothing that training cannot do. Nothing is above its reach or below it.

—"As Regards Patriotism" essay, written about 1900

The self taught man seldom knows anything accurately, and he does not know a tenth as much as he could have known if he had worked under teachers, and besides, he brags, and is the means of fooling other thoughtless people into going and doing as he himself has done.

—"Taming the Bicycle"

We never knew an ignorant person yet but was prejudiced.

—*The Innocents Abroad* (1869)

In the first place God made idiots. This was for practice. Then He made school boards.

—*Following the Equator* (1897)

Now then, to me university degrees are unearned finds, and they bring the joy that belongs with property acquired in that way; and the money-finds and the degree-finds are just the same in number up to date— three: two from Yale and one from Missouri University. It pleased me beyond measure when Yale made me a Master of Arts, because I didn't know anything about art; I had another convulsion of pleasure when Yale made me a Doctor of Literature, because I was not competent to doctor anybody's literature but my own, and couldn't even keep my own in a healthy condition without my wife's help. I rejoiced again when Missouri University made me a Doctor of Laws, because it was all clear profit, I not knowing anything about laws except how to evade them and not get caught. And now at Oxford I am to be made a Doctor of Letters—all clear profit, because what I don't know about letters would make me a mutli-millionaire if I could turn it into cash.

—*Autobiography*

By advice, I turned my attention to the Greek department. I told the Greek professor I had concluded to drop the use of the Greek written character, because it was so hard to spell with, and so impossible to read after you get it spelled. Let us draw the curtain there. I saw by what followed that nothing but early neglect saved him from being a very profane man.

—1889 speech

I ordered the professor of mathematics to simplify the whole system . . . we didn't want any more cases of *if* A and B stand at opposite poles of the earth's surface and C at the equator of Jupiter, at what variations of angle will the left limb of the moon appear to these different parties? I said you just let that thing alone; it's plenty time to get in a sweat about it when it happens; as like as not it ain't going to do any harm anyway.

—1889 speech

I found the astronomer of the university gadding around after comets and other such odds and ends— tramps and derelicts of the skies. I told him pretty plainly that we couldn't have that. I told him it was no economy to go on piling up and piling up raw material in the way of new stars and comets and asteroids that we couldn't ever have any use for till we had worked off the old stock.

—1889 speech

Many public-school children seem to know only two dates—1492 and 4th of July; and as a rule they don't know what happened on either occasion.

—"The Game"

Every time you stop a school, you will have to build a jail. What you gain at one end you lose at the other. It's like feeding a dog on his own tail. It won't fatten the dog.

—1900 speech

It is noble to teach oneself, but still nobler to teach others—and less trouble.

—1906 speech

CHAPTER FOURTEEN

"The American Lion of St. Mark's," from
Life magazine (1901)

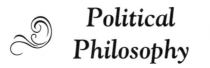 **Political Philosophy**

No, we are not going to ignore those two subjects you always were told to ignore—politics and religion. Mark Twain just had too much sound advice on both topics. And we happen to be in desperate need of sanity on these topics. First up is politics, and we'd all be on a better road if we followed Mark Twain's guidance in this tricky territory.

Yes, you are right—I am a moralist in disguise; it gets me into heaps of trouble when I go thrashing around in political questions.

—1902 letter

If the man doesn't believe as we do, we say he is a crank, and that settles it. I mean, it does nowadays, because now we can't burn him.

—*Following the Equator* (1897)

Men think they think upon the great political questions, and they do; but they think with their party, not independently; they read its literature, but not that of the other side.

—"Corn-pone Opinions"

You see my kind of loyalty was loyalty to one's country, not to its institutions, or its office holders. The country is the real thing, the substantial thing, the eternal thing; it is the thing to watch over, and care for, and be loyal to; institutions are extraneous, they are its mere clothing, and clothing can wear out, become ragged, cease to be comfortable, cease to protect the body from winter, disease, and death. To be loyal to rags, to shout for rags, to worship rags, to die for rags—this is loyalty to unreason, it is pure animal; it belongs to monarchy, was invented by monarchy; let monarchy keep it.

—*A Connecticut Yankee in King Arthur's Court* (1889)

The citizen who thinks he sees that the commonwealth's political clothes are worn out, and yet holds his peace and does not agitate for a new suit, is disloyal; he is a traitor.

—*A Connecticut Yankee in King Arthur's Court* (1889)

St. Patrick had no politics; his sympathies lay with the right—that was politics enough. When he came across a reptile, he forgot to inquire whether he was a Democrat or a Republican, but simply exalted his staff and "let him have it."

—1876 letter

Every citizen of the republic ought to consider himself an unofficial policeman, and keep unsalaried watch and ward over the laws and their execution.

—"Traveling With a Reformer"

Citizenship should be placed above everything else, even learning. Is there in any college of the land a chair of citizenship where good citizenship and all that it implies is taught? There is not one—that is, not one where sane citizenship is taught. There are some which teach insane citizenship, bastard citizenship, but that is all. Patriotism! Yes; but patriotism is usually the refuge of the scoundrel. He is the man who talks the loudest.

—1908 speech

Citizenship is what makes a republic; monarchies can get along without it.

—1906 speech

For in a republic, who is "the Country"? Is it the Government which is for the moment in the saddle? Why, the Government is merely a servant—merely a temporary servant; it cannot be its prerogative to determine what is right and what is wrong, and decide who is a patriot and who isn't. Its function is to obey orders, not originate them. Who, then, is "the Country"? Is it the newspaper? Is it the pulpit?

Is it the school superintendent? Why, these are mere parts of the country, not the whole of it; they have not command, they have only their little share in the command. They are but one in a thousand; it is in the thousand that command is lodged; they must determine what is right and what is wrong; they must decide who is a patriot and who isn't.

—"Papers of the Adam Family"

We teach them to take their patriotism at second-hand; to shout with the largest crowd without examining into the right or wrong of the matter—exactly as boys under monarchies are taught and have always been taught. We teach them to regard as traitors, and hold in aversion and contempt, such as do not shout with the crowd, and so here in our democracy we are cheering a thing which of all things is most foreign to it and out of place—the delivery of our political conscience into somebody else's keeping. This is patriotism on the Russian plan.

—quoted in *Mark Twain: A Biography* (1912)
by Albert Bigelow Paine

Loyalty to petrified opinion never yet broke a chain or freed a human soul in this world—and never will.

—1887 speech

These same men who enthusiastically preach loyal consistency to church and party are always ready and willing and anxious to persuade a Chinaman or an Indian or a Kanaka to desert *his* church, or a fellow-American to desert *his* party. The man who deserts to them is all that is high and pure and beautiful—apparently; the man who deserts from them is all that is foul and despicable. This is Consistency with a capital C.

—1887 speech

What is the most rigorous law of our being? Growth. No smallest atom of our moral, mental, or physical structure can stand still a year. It *grows*. It must grow; nothing can prevent it . . . it cannot stand still. In other words, we change—and must change, constantly, and keep on changing as long as we live. What, then, is the true gospel of consistency? Change. Who is the really consistent man? The man who changes. Since change is the law of his being, he cannot *be* consistent if he sticks in a rut. Yet . . . there are those who would misteach us that to stick in a rut is consistency—and a virtue; and that to climb out of the rut is inconsistency—and a vice.

—1887 speech

I am persuaded that the world has been tricked into adopting some false and most pernicious notions about consistency—and to such a degree that the average man has turned the rights and wrongs of things entirely around and is proud to be "consistent," unchanging, immovable, fossilized, where it should be his humiliation that he is so.

—1887 speech

Whenever you find yourself on the side of the majority, it is time to reform (or pause and reflect).

—1904 notebook entry

It were not best that we should all think alike; it is difference of opinion that makes horse races.

—*Pudd'nhead Wilson* (1894)

The new party member who supposed himself independent will presently find that the party has somehow got a mortgage on his soul, and that within a year he will recognize the mortgage, deliver up his liberty, and actually believe he cannot retire from the party from any motive, however high and right, in his own eye, without shame and dishonor. Is it possible for human wickedness to invent a doctrine more infernal and poisonous than this? What slave is so degraded as the slave who is *proud* that he is a slave?

—1887 speech

This atrocious doctrine of allegiance to party plays directly into the hands of politicians of the baser sort . . . for they know that the docile party will vote for any forked thing they put up, even though it does not even strictly resemble a man.

—1887 speech

If we would learn what the human race really is at bottom, we need only observe it in election times.

—*Autobiography*

Without a blush he will vote for an unclean boss if that boss is the party's Moses, without compunction he will vote against the best man in the whole land if he is on the other ticket.

—1906 speech

No party holds the privilege of dictating to me how I shall vote. If loyalty to party is a form of patriotism, I am no patriot. If there is any valuable difference between a monarchist and an American, it lies in the theory that the American can decide for himself what is patriotic and what isn't. I claim that difference. I am the only person in the sixty millions that is privileged to dictate my patriotism.

—quoted in *Mark Twain: A Biography* (1912)
by Albert Bigelow Paine

I have said there that when Europe gets a ruler lodged in her gullet, there is no help for it but a bloody revolution; here we go and get a great big, emetical ballot, and heave it up.

—1889 interview

Good citizenship would teach accuracy of thinking and accuracy of statement.

—1908 speech

That's the difference between governments and individuals. Governments don't care, individuals do.

—*A Tramp Abroad* (1880)

No country can be well governed unless its citizens as a body keep religiously before their minds that they are the guardians of the law and that the law officers are only the machinery for its execution, nothing more.

—*The Gilded Age* (1873)

Suppose you were an idiot. And suppose you were a member of Congress. But I repeat myself.

—quoted in *Mark Twain: A Biography* (1912) by Albert Bigelow Paine

It could probably be shown by facts and figures that there is no distinctly native American criminal class except Congress.

—*Following the Equator* (1897)

History has tried hard to teach us that we can't have good government under politicians. Now, to go and stick one at the very head of the government couldn't be wise.

—quoted in the *New York Herald* (1876)

I think I can say, and say with pride, that we have some legislatures that bring higher prices than any in the world.

—1873 speech

An honest man in politics shines more than he would elsewhere.

—*A Tramp Abroad* (1880)

The lightning there is peculiar; it is so convincing, that when it strikes a thing it doesn't leave enough of that thing behind for you to tell whether—well, you'd think it was something valuable, and a Congressman had been there.

—1876 speech

There is something good and motherly about Washington, the grand old benevolent National Asylum for the helpless.

—*The Gilded Age* (1873)

But above all and beyond all, it can be said with entire sincerity, the he is a square, honest man—a square, honest man in politics, think of that—and I will remark here, in confidence, that he occupies an almighty lonesome position.

—1879 speech

All Congresses and Parliaments have a kindly feeling for idiots, and a compassion for them, on account of personal experience and heredity.

—*Autobiography*

The government of my country snubs honest simplic- ity, but fondles artistic villainy, and I think I might have developed into a very capable pickpocket if I had remained in the public service a year or two.

—*Roughing It* (1872)

Whiskey is carried into committee rooms in demi-johns [large bottle with narrow neck] and carried out in demagogues.

—1868 notebook entry

It is curious—curious that physical courage should be so common in the world, and moral courage so rare.

—*Mark Twain in Eruption* (1940)

The human race is a race of cowards; and I am not only marching in that procession but carrying a banner.

—*Mark Twain in Eruption* (1940)

I have never made but one political speech before this. That was years ago. I made a logical, closely reasoned, compact, powerful argument against a discriminating and iniquitous tax which was about to be imposed by the opposition—I may say I made a most thoughtful, symmetrical, and admirable argument; but a Michigan newspaper editor answered it—refuted it—utterly demolished it—by saying I was in the constant habit of horsewhipping my great grandmother.

—1879 speech

I don't mind what the opposition say of me so long as they don't tell the truth about me. But when they descend to telling the truth about me I consider that this is taking an unfair advantage.

—1879 speech

The ablest newspaper in Colorado—the ablest news-paper in the world—has recently nominated me for President . . . If I had realized that this canvass was to turn on the candidate's private character, I would have started that Colorado paper sooner. I know the crimes that can be imputed and proved against me can be told on the fingers of your hands—not all your hands, but only just simply the most of them. This cannot be said of any other presidential candidate in the field.

—1884 speech

The radical of one century is the conservative of the next. The radical invents the views. When he has worn them out the conservative adopts them.

—1898 notebook

Here I was, in a country where a right to say how the country should be governed was restricted to six persons in each thousand of its population . . . I was become a stockholder in a corporation where nine hundred and ninety-four of the members furnished all the money and did all the work, and the other six elected themselves a permanent board of directors and took all the dividends. It seemed to me that what the nine hundred and ninety-four dupes needed was a new deal.

—*A Connecticut Yankee in King Arthur's Court* (1889)

I shall not often meddle with politics, because we have a political Editor who is already excellent and only needs to serve a term or two in the penitentiary to be perfect.

—quoted in *Mark Twain: A Biography* (1912)
by Albert Bigelow Paine

CHAPTER FIFTEEN

HIGH CHURCH.

from *A Connecticut Yankee in
King Arthur's Court* (1889)

Religious Matters

One of Mark Twain's very closest friends (for more than forty years) was the Reverend Joseph Hopkins Twichell. Obviously, there was much on which they agreed to disagree. But, believe it, the gospel according to Mark (Twain, that is) contains much sound guidance for believers and non-believers. You don't need to take this on faith; Brother Mark is about to enlighten us:

So much blood has been shed by the Church because of an omission from the Gospel: "Ye shall be indifferent as to what your neighbor's religion is." Not merely tolerant of it, but indifferent to it. Divinity is claimed for many religions; but no religion is great enough or divine enough to add that new law to its code.

—quoted in *Mark Twain: A Biography* (1912)
by Albert Bigelow Paine

Man is a Religious Animal. He is the only Religious Animal. He is the only animal that has the True Religion—several of them. He is the only animal that loves his neighbor as himself and cuts his throat if his theology isn't straight. He has made a graveyard of the globe in trying his honest best to smooth his brother's path to happiness and heaven . . . The higher animals have no religion. And we are told that they are going to be left out in the Hereafter. I wonder why? It seems questionable taste.

—"The Lowest Animal"

You cain't pray a lie.

—*Adventures of Huckleberry Finn* (1885)

But we were good boys, good Presbyterian boys, all Presbyterian boys, and loyal and all that; anyway, we were good Presbyterian boys when the weather was doubtful; when it was fair, we did wander a little from the fold.

—1902 speech

Man was made at the end of the week's work when God was tired.

—*Mark Twain's Notebook* (1935)

Indeed, none but the Deity can tell what is good luck and what is bad before the returns are all in.

—1904 letter

Humor must be one of the chief attributes of God. Plants and animals that are distinctly humorous in form and characteristics are God's jokes.

—quoted in *Mark Twain: A Biography* (1912)
by Albert Bigelow Paine

True irreverence is disrespect for another man's god.

—*Following the Equator* (1897)

There was no crime. Merely little things like pillaging orchards and watermelon patches and breaking the Sabbath—we didn't break the Sabbath often enough to signify—once a week perhaps.

—1902 speech

Mine was a trained Presbyterian conscience and knew but the one duty—to hunt and harry its slave upon all pretexts and on all occasions, particularly when there was no sense nor reason in it.

—*Autobiography*

The Christian's Bible is a drug store. Its contents remain the same; but the medical practice changes . . . During many ages there were witches. The Bible said so. The Bible commanded that they should not be allowed to live. Therefore the Church, after eight hundred years, gathered up its halters, thumb-screws, and firebrands, and set about its holy work in earnest. She worked hard at it night and day during nine centuries and imprisoned, tortured, hanged, and burned whole hordes and armies of witches, and washed the Christian world clean with their foul blood.

Then it was discovered that there was no such thing as witches, and never had been. One does not know whether to laugh or to cry . . . There are no witches. The witch text remains; only the practice has changed. Hell fire is gone, but the text remains. Infant damnation is gone, but the text remains. More than two hundred death penalties are gone from the law books, but the texts that authorized them remain.

—*Europe and Elsewhere* (1923)

There are those who scoff at the school boy, calling him frivolous and shallow. Yet it was the school boy who said, Faith is believing what you know ain't so.

—*Following the Equator* (1897)

There has been only one Christian. They caught him and crucified him—early.

—1898 notebook entry

If Christ were here there is one thing he would not be—a Christian.

—*Mark Twain's Notebook* (1935)

Blasphemy? No, it is not blasphemy. If God is as vast as that, he is above blasphemy; if He is as little as that, He is beneath it.

—quoted in *Mark Twain: A Biography* (1912)
by Albert Bigelow Paine

I am plenty safe enough in his hands; I am not in any danger from that kind of a Diety. The one that I want to keep out of the reach of, is the caricature of him which one finds in the Bible. We (that one and I) could never respect each other, never get along together. I have met his superior a hundred times—in fact I amount to that myself.

—1889 letter

The church is always trying to get other people to reform; it might not be a bad idea to reform itself a little, by way of example.

—*A Tramp Abroad* (1880)

I believe our Heavenly Father invented man because he was disappointed in the monkey.

—*Mark Twain in Eruption*

Such is the human race. Often it does seem such a pity that Noah and his party did not miss the boat.

—*Christian Science* (1907)

He didn't know nothing at all the rest of the day, and preached a prayer-meeting sermon that night that give him a rattling reputation, because the oldest man in the world couldn't a understood it.

—*Adventures of Huckleberry Finn* (1885)

The choir always tittered and whispered all through the service. There was once a church choir that was not ill-bred, but I have forgotten where it was.

—*The Adventures of Tom Sawyer* (1876)

I have been reading the morning paper. I do it every morning—knowing well that I shall find in it the usual depravities and basenesses and hypocrisies and cruelties that make up civilization, and cause me to put in the rest of the day pleading for the damnation of the human race. I cannot seem to get my prayers answered, yet I do not despair.

—1899 letter

Nothing agrees with me. If I drink coffee, it gives me dyspepsia; if I drink wine, it gives me the gout; if I go to church, it gives me dysentery.

—1905 letter

Man is the only animal that deals in that atrocity of atrocities, War. He is the only one that gathers his brethren about him and goes forth in cold blood . . . to exterminate his kind. He is the only animal that for sordid wages will march out . . . and help to slaughter strangers of his own species who have done him no harm and with whom he has no quarrel . . . And in the intervals between campaigns he washes the blood off his hands and works for "the universal brotherhood of man"—with mouth.

—*What Is Man?*

The noblest work of God? Man. Who found it out? Man.

—*Autobiography*

There are times when one would like to hang the whole human race, and finish the farce.

—*A Connecticut Yankee in King Arthur's Court* (1889)

I am the only man living who understands human nature; God has put me in charge of this branch office; when I retire there will be no-one to take my place. I shall keep on doing my duty, for when I get over on the other side, I shall use my influence to have the human race drowned again, and this time drowned good, no omissions, no Ark.

—quoted in J. Macy's *Mark Twain* (1913)

There are two kinds of Christian morals, one private and the other public. These two are so distinct, so unrelated, that they are no more akin to each other than are archangels and politicians.

—1906 speech

It now seems plain to me that that theory ought to be vacated in favor of a new and truer one . . . the Descent of Man from the Higher Animals.

—"The Lowest Animal"

A sin takes on a new and real terror when there seems a chance that it is going to be found out.

—"The Man That Corrupted Hadleyburg"

What is courtesy? Consideration for others. Is there a good deal of it in the American character? So far as I have observed, no. Is it an American characteristic? So far as I have observed, the most prominent, the most American of all American characteristics, is the poverty of it in the American character.

—1906 speech

As by the fires of experience, so by commission of crime you learn real morals. Commit all crimes, familiarize yourself with all sins, take them in rotation (there are only two or three thousand of them), stick to it, commit two or three every day, and by and by you will be proof against them. When you are through you will be proof against all sins and morally perfect. You will be vaccinated against every possible commission of them. This is the only way.

—1899 speech

An injurious truth has no merit over an injurious lie . . . a great soul, with a great purpose, can make a weak body strong and keep it so.

—*Personal Recollections of Joan of Arc* (1896)

What have we done for Adam? Nothing. What has Adam done for us? Everything. He gave us life, he gave us death, he gave us heaven, he gave us hell. These are inestimable privileges—and remember, not one of them should we have without Adam. Well, then, he ought to have a monument.

—*New York Times*, 1883

Man is kind enough when he is not excited by religion.

—"A Horse's Tale"

One mustn't criticize other people on grounds where he can't stand perpendicular himself.

—*A Connecticut Yankee in King Arthur's Court* (1889)

We despise all reverences and all the objects of reverence which are outside the pale of our own list of sacred things. And yet, with strange inconsistency, we are shocked when other people despise and defile the things which are holy to us.

—*Following the Equator* (1897)

It is a civilization which has destroyed the simplicity
and repose of life; replaced its contentment, its poetry,
its soft romance-dreams and visions with the mon-
ey-fever, sordid ideals, vulgar ambitions, and the sleep
which does not refresh; it has invented a thousand
useless luxuries, and turned them into necessities; it
has created a thousand vicious appetites and satisfies
none of them; it has dethroned God and set up a shekel
in His place.

—"Papers of the Adam Family"

The easy confidence with which I know another man's
religion is folly teaches me to suspect that my own
is also. I would not interfere with any one's religion,
either to strengthen it or to weaken it. I am not able
to believe one's religion can affect his hereafter one
way or the other, no matter what that religion may
be. But it may easily be a great comfort to him in this
life—hence it is a valuable possession to him.

—quoted in *Mark Twain: A Biography* (1912)
by Albert Bigelow Paine

Neither should ever be uttered. The man who speaks an injurious truth, lest his soul be not saved if he do otherwise, should reflect that that sort of a soul is not strictly worth saving.

—"On the Decay of the Art of Lying"

Being made merely in the image of God, but not otherwise resembling him enough to be mistaken by anybody but a very near-sighted person.

—letter to his sister, Pamela (undated)

Ah, well, I am a great and sublime fool. But then I am God's fool, and all His work must be contemplated with respect.

—quoted in *Mark Twain: A Biography* (1912)
by Albert Bigelow Paine

CHAPTER SIXTEEN

THE ROBBERS DISPERSED

from *Adventures of Huckleberry Finn* (1885)

Surviving Childhood

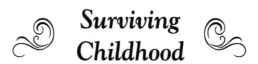

Few writers were as in touch with their inner child. Mark Twain never lost the ability to relate to children, and his own childhood was quickly recalled in remarkable detail. When most adults become parents, they defect to "the other side." Twain remained in both camps, alive to the joys and fears of each world.

Always obey your parents, when they are present.

> —"Advice to Young People" speech (1882)

Most parents think they know better than you do, and you can generally make more by humoring that supposition than you can by acting on your own better judgment.

> —"Advice to Young People" speech (1882)

You ought never to "sass" old people—unless they "sass" you first.

> —"Advice for Good Little Girls"

You ought never to take anything that don't belong to you—if you cannot carry it off.

> —"Advice for Good Little Boys"

We ought never to do wrong when people are looking.

> —"A Double-Barrelled Detective Story"

Be respectful to your superiors, if you have any.

> —"Advice to Young People" speech (1882)

You should never do anything wicked and lay it on your brother, when it is just as convenient to lay it on some other boy.

—"Advice for Good Little Boys"

When in doubt, tell the truth.

—*Following the Equator* (1897)

Now as to the matter of lying. You want to be very careful about lying; otherwise you are nearly sure to get caught.

—"Advice to Young People" speech (1882)

An awkward, feeble, leaky lie is a thing which you ought to make your unceasing study to avoid; such a lie as that has no more real permanence than an average truth. Why, you might as well tell the truth at once and be done with it. A feeble, stupid, preposterous lie will not live two years—except it be a slander upon somebody. It is indestructible then.

—"Advice to Young People" speech (1882)

Some authorities hold that the young ought not to lie at all. That, of course, is putting it rather stronger than necessary; still, while I cannot go quite so far as that, I do maintain, and I believe I am right, that the young ought to be temperate in the use of this great art until practice and experience shall give them the confidence, elegance, and precision which alone can make the accomplishment graceful and profitable.

—"Advice to Young People" speech (1882)

Do not put off until tomorrow what can be put off till day-after-tomorrow just as well.

—quoted in *More Maxims of Mark* (1927),
edited by M. Johnson

There are people who think that honesty is always the best policy. This is a superstition. There are times when the appearance of it is worth six of it.

—*Following the Equator* (1897)

Adam and Eve had many advantages, but the principle one was that they escaped teething.

—*Pudd'nhead Wilson* (1894)

When a teacher calls a boy by his entire name it means trouble.

—*Mark Twain in Eruption* (1940)

Always avoid violence; in this age of charity and kind-liness, the time has gone by for such things. Leave dynamite to the low and unrefined.

—"Advice to Young People" speech (1882)

Always acknowledge a fault frankly. This will throw those in authority off their guard and give you oppor-tunity to commit more.

—quoted in *More Maxims of Mark* (1927),
edited by M. Johnson

If your mother tells you do a thing, it is wrong to reply that you won't. It is better and more becoming to intimate that you will do as she bids you, and then afterwards act quietly in the matter according to the dictates of your better judgment.

—"Advice for Good Little Girls"

It is at our mother's knee that we acquire our noblest and truest and highest ideals, but there is seldom any money in them.

—quoted in *Mark Twain: A Biography* (1912)
by Albert Bigelow Paine

She merely gave me a crack on the skull with her thimble that I felt all the way down to my heels. Then I broke out with my injured innocence . . . She said without emotion, "It's all right. It isn't any matter. You deserve it for something you've done that I didn't know about; and if you haven't done it, why then you deserve it for something that you are going to do, that I shan't hear about."

—*Autobiography*

What's the use you learning to do right when it's troublesome to do right and ain't no trouble to do wrong, and the wages is just the same?

—*Adventures of Huckleberry Finn* (1885)

Good little girls ought not to make mouths at their teachers for every trifling offense. This retaliation should be resorted to under peculiarly aggravating circumstances.

—"Advice for Good Little Girls"

If at any time you find it necessary to correct your brother, do not correct him with mud—never, on any account, throw mud at him, because it will spoil his clothes. It is better to scald him a little, for then you obtain desirable results—you secure his immediate attention to the lesson you are inculcating, and at the same time your hot water will have a tendency to move impurities from his person—and possibly the skin also, in spots.

—"Advice for Good Little Girls"

If you unthinkingly set up a tack in another boy's seat, you ought never to laugh when he sits down on it—unless you can't "hold in."

—"Advice for Good Little Boys"

You ought never to call your aged grandpapa a "rum old file"—except when you want to be unusually funny.

—"Advice for Good Little Boys"

The Model Boy of my time—we never had but the one—was perfect: perfect in manners, perfect in dress, perfect in conduct, perfect in filial piety, perfect in filial godliness; but at bottom he was a prig; and as for the contents of his skull, they could have changed place with the contents of a pie, and nobody would have been the worse off for it but the pie. This fellow's reproachlessness was a standing reproach to every lad in the village. He was the admiration of all the mothers, and the detestation of all their sons.

—*Life on the Mississippi* (1883)

One is not blameable for mistakes, we all make them. A mistake is not a crime, it is only a miscarriage of judgment.

—1908 letter

And that is one of the very advantages of youth. You don't own any stock in anything. You have a good time, and all the grief and trouble is with the other fellows.

—1895 speech

Youth is a lovely thing, and certainly never was there a diviner time to me in this world.

—1895 speech

It is good to obey all the rules when you're young, so you'll have the strength to break them when you're old.

—quoted in 1940 article by Dorothy Quick

CHAPTER SEVENTEEN

THE GRACE OF A KANGAROO.

from *Roughing It* (1872)

Romance
 &
Marriage

Four days after marrying Olivia Langdon in February 1870, Mark Twain wrote to a friend, "She is the very most perfect gem of womankind that ever I saw in my life—& I will stand by that remark till I die." He did. Two years before Livy's death in June 1904, he told a New York audience, "She has been the best friend I have ever had, and that is saying a good deal."

This 4th of February will be the mightiest day in the history of our lives, the holiest, & the most generous toward us both—for it makes of two fractional lives a whole; it gives to two purposeless lives a work, & doubles the strength of each whereby to perform it; it gives to two questioning natures a reason for living, & something to live for; it will give a new gladness to the sunshine, a new fragrance to the flowers, a new beauty to the earth, a new mystery to life; & Livy it will give a new revelation to love, a new depth to sorrow, a new impulse to worship. In that day the scales will fall from our eyes & we shall look upon a new world. Speed it!

—September 1869 letter to his
fiancée, Olivia Langdon

People talk about beautiful friendships between two persons of the same sex. What is the best of that sort, as compared with the friendship of man and wife, where the best impulses and highest ideals of both are the same. There is no place for comparison between the two friendships; the one is earthly, the other divine.

—*A Connecticut Yankee in King Arthur's Court* (1889)

Love seems the swiftest, but it is the slowest of all growths. No man or woman really knows what perfect love is until they have been married a quarter of a century.

—*Mark Twain's Notebook* (1935)

When you fish for love, bait with your heart, not your brain.

—1898 notebook entry

You can't reason with your heart; it has its own laws, and thumps about things which the intellect scorns.

—*A Connecticut Yankee in King Arthur's Court* (1889)

Courtship lifts a young fellow far and away above his common earthly self and by an impulse natural to those lofty regions he puts on his halo and his heavenly war paint and plays archangel as if he were born to it. He is working a deception, but is not aware of it.

—"Which Was the Dream"

Chastity, you can carry it too far.

—1907 speech

There isn't time—so brief is life—for bickerings, apologies, heartburnings, callings to account. There is only time for loving—& but an instant, so to speak, for that.

—1886 letter

Thou shalt not commit adultry is a command which makes no distinction between the following persons. They are all required to obey it: children at birth. Children in the cradle. School children. Youths and maidens. Fresh adults. Older ones. Men and women of 40. Of 50. Of 60. Of 70. Of 80. Of 100. The command does not distribute its burden equally, and cannot. It is not hard upon the three sets of children.

—*Letters from the Earth* (1962)

The adultery law [in Hawaii] has been so amended that each party to the offense is now fined thirty dollars; and I would remark, in passing, that if the crime were invariably detected and the fines collected, the revenues of the Hawaiian Government would probably exceed those of the United States.

—1866 letter

Love is not a product of reasonings and statistics. It just comes—none knows whence—and cannot explain itself.

—*Eve's Diary* (1905)

After all these years, I see that I was mistaken about Eve in the beginning; it is better to live outside the Garden with her than inside it without her.

—*Extracts from Adam's Diary* (1893)

Wheresoever she was, there was Eden.

—Adam's addendum to *Eve's Diary* (1905)

CHAPTER EIGHTEEN

from *Sketches New and Old* (1875)

Parenthood

*Mark Twain as a parent to three daughters (Susy, Clara, and Jean)?
We again consult the biography Susy began at thirteen: "He does
tell perfectly delightful stories. Clara and I used to sit on each arm
of his chair and listen while he told us stories about the pictures on
the wall." The children often would bring him a magazine with a
picture and require him to instantly build a story around it. Clara
once requested a story about a plumber and a "bawgun strictor."
As Twain later recalled, "She didn't know what a boa constrictor
was until he developed in the tale—then she was better satisfied
with it than ever."*

Familiarity breeds contempt—and children.

—1894 notebook entry

It is a wise child that knows its own father, and an unusual one that unreservedly approves of him.

—quoted in *More Maxims of Mark* (1927),
edited by M. Johnson

The proverb says that Providence protects children and idiots. This is really true. I know because I have tested it.

—*Autobiography*

The most useful and interesting letters we get here from home are from children seven or eight years old. This is petrified truth. Happily they have got nothing to talk about but home, and neighbours and family—things their betters think unworthy of transmission thousands of miles. They write simply and naturally, and without straining for effect. They tell all they know, and then stop.

—"An Open Letter to the American People" (1866)

I thought this was a home. It was a superstition. What is a home without a child?

—August 1907 letter

Children have but little charity for one another's defects.

—*Autobiography*

We think boys are rude, unsensitive animals but it is not so in all cases. Each boy has one or two sensitive spots, and if you can find out where they are located you have only to touch them and you can scorch him as with fire.

—*Autobiography*

This curious & pathetic fact of life: that when parents are old & their children grown up, the grown-up children are not the persons they formerly were; that their former selves have wandered away, never to return again, save in dream-glimpses of their young forms that tarry a moment & gladden the eye, then vanish & break the heart.

—Memorial to Olivia Susan Clemens

The darling mispronunciations of childhood!—dear me, there's no music that can touch it; and how one grieves when it wastes away and dissolves into correct-ness, knowing it will never visit his bereaved ear again.

—*A Connecticut Yankee in King Arthur's Court* (1889)

If you will go back fifty or one hundred years to your early married life and recontemplate your first baby—you will remember that he amounted to a good deal . . . You soldiers all know that when that little fellow arrived at family headquarters you had to hand in your resignation. He took entire command. You became his lackey, his mere body-servant, and you had to stand around, too. He was not a commander who made allowances for time, distance, weather, or anything else. You had to execute his order whether it was possible or not. And there was only one form of marching in his manual of tactics, and that was the double-quick. He treated you with every sort of insolence and disrespect, and the bravest of you didn't dare to say a word.

—"The Babies" speech (1879)

Sentimental young folks still take stock in that beautiful old saying that when the baby smiles in his sleep, it is because the angels are whispering to him . . . simply wind on the stomach, my friends.

—"The Babies" speech (1879)

One baby can furnish more business than you and your whole Interior Department can attend to. He is enterprising, irrepressible, brimful of lawless activities.

—"The Babies" speech (1879)

I don't like this thing of being stripped naked & washed. I like to be stripped & warmed at the stove—that is real bully—but I do despise this washing business. I believe it to be a gratuitous & unnecessary piece of meanness. I never see them wash the cat.

—1870 letter written in the voice
of his infant son, Langdon

A baby is an inestimable blessing and bother.

—1876 letter

CHAPTER NINETEEN

PAINTING MY GREAT PICTURE.

from *A Tramp Abroad* (1880)

Reaching Old Age, Finding Wisdom

The writer we know as Mark Twain was known by different names to the many different people in his crowded life. Boyhood pals knew him as Sam. Close friends William Dean Howells and Henry Huttleston Rogers called him Clemens (as he referred to them as Howells and Rogers). To an equally close friend, Congregationalist pastor Joseph Hopkins Twichell, he was Mark. To his three loving daughters, he was Papa. But his wife, Livy, called him Youth. Howells believed this suited him, saying his friend possessed "the heart of a boy with the head of a sage." What better source for the rules of the road as we travel toward age and wisdom? And the first rule on the next page is one to carry around with you and make you feel, in Twain's words, "as good as church letting out."

Wrinkles should merely indicate where smiles have been.

—Following the Equator (1897)

How stunning are the changes which age makes in a man while he sleeps!

—1887 letter

I have achieved my seventy years in the usual way; by sticking to a scheme of life which would kill anybody else . . . I will offer here, as a sound maxim, this: That we can't reach old age by another man's road . . . My habits protect my life, but they would assassinate you.

—1905 speech

Lord save us all from old age and broken health and a hope tree that has lost the faculty of putting out blossoms.

—1891 letter

I haven't a particle of confidence in a man who has no redeeming petty vices.

—quoted in *Mark Twain: A Biography* (1912)
by Albert Bigelow Paine

Change is the handmaiden Nature requires to do her miracles with.

—*Roughing It* (1872)

I am too old to learn, but I am not too old to teach.

—1901 speech

It was on the 10th day of May [1884] . . . I confessed to age by mounting spectacles for the first time, and in the same hour I renewed my youth, to outward appearance, by mounting a bicycle for the first time. The spectacles stayed on.

—1884 speech

It is in the heart that the values lie. I wish I could make him understand that a loving heart is riches, and riches enough, and that without it intellect is poverty.

—*Eve's Diary* (1905)

A human being has a natural desire to have more of a good thing than he needs.

—*Following the Equator* (1897)

I am aware that I am very old now; but I am also aware that I have never been so young as I am now, in spirit . . . I am only able to perceive that I am old by a mental process; I am altogether unable to feel old in spirit . . . When I am in the company of very young people I always feel that I am one of them, and they probably privately resent it.

—1906 autobiographical dictation

Life was a fairy-tale, then, it is a tragedy now. When I was 43 and John Hay 41 he said life was a tragedy after 40, and I disputed it. Three years ago he asked me to testify again: I counted my graves, and there was nothing for me to say. I am old; I recognize it but I don't realize it. I wonder if a person ever really ceases to feel young—I mean, for a whole day at a time.

—1906 letter

It is the epitome of life. The first half of it consists of the capacity to enjoy without the chance; the last half consists of the chance without the capacity.

—1901 letter

The calamity that comes is never the one we had prepared ourselves for.

—1896 letter

Life should begin with age and its privileges and accumulations, and end with youth and its capacity to splendidly enjoy such advantages.

—1901 letter

Seventy is old enough. After that there is too much risk.
—*Following the Equator* (1897)

It isn't so astonishing, the number of things that I can remember, as the number of things I can remember that aren't so.

—quoted in *Mark Twain: A Biography* (1912)
by Albert Bigelow Paine

When I was younger I could remember anything, whether it happened or not; but I am getting old, and soon I shall remember only the latter.

—quoted in *Mark Twain: A Biography* (1912)
by Albert Bigelow Paine

Why is it that we rejoice at a birth and grieve at a funeral? It is because we are not the person involved.

—*Pudd'nhead Wilson* (1894)

The Moral Sense teaches us what is right, and how to avoid it—when unpopular.

—"The United States of Lyncherdom"

I was young and foolish then; now I am old and foolisher.

—quoted in *Mark Twain: A Biography* (1912)
by Albert Bigelow Paine

There is no character, howsoever good and fine, but it can be destroyed by ridicule, howsoever poor and witless. Observe the ass, for instance: his character is about perfect, he is the choicest spirit among all the humbler animals, yet see what ridicule has brought him to.

—*Pudd'nhead Wilson* (1894)

Necessity is the mother of taking chances.

—*Roughing It* (1872)

Always do right. This will gratify some people, and astonish the rest.

—1901 note

Be good and you will be lonesome.

—*Following the Equator* (1897)

It is very wearing to be good.

—*Life on the Mississippi* (1883)

All good things arrive unto them that wait—and don't die in the meantime.

—1889 letter

The heart is the real Fountain of Youth. While that remains young the Waterbury of Time must stand still.

—1898 notebook entry

To arrive at a just estimate of a renowned man's character one must judge it by the standards of his time, not ours.

—*Personal Recollections of Joan of Arc* (1896)

When a person cannot deceive himself the chances are against his being able to deceive other people.

—Autobiography

I said there was but one solitary thing about the past worth remembering and that was the fact that it is past—can't be restored.

—1876 letter

Everyone is a moon, and has a dark side which he never shows to anybody.

—Following the Equator (1897)

We find not much in ourselves to admire, we are always privately wanting to be like somebody else. If everybody was satisfied with himself there would be no heroes.

—Autobiography

In my age, as in my youth, night brings me many a deep remorse. I realize that from the cradle up I have been like the rest of the race—never quite sane in the night.

—Autobiography

It is not in the least likely that any life has ever been lived which was not a failure in the secret judgment of the person who lived it.

—*Mark Twain's Notebook* (1935)

There is no sadder sight than a young pessimist, except an old optimist.

—quoted in *More Maxims of Mark* (1927),
edited by M. Johnson

Praise is well, compliment is well, but affection—that is the last and final and most precious reward that any man can win, whether by character or achievement.

—Speech, 1907

Let us endeavor so to live that when we come to die even the undertaker will be sorry.

—*Pudd'nhead Wilson* (1894)

CHAPTER TWENTY

A CURIOUS DREAM.

from *Sketches New and Old* (1875)

The End
of the Road?

Mark Twain made it to seventy-four—all in all, not a bad run for that time. Perhaps by modifying his habits a bit more, he would have given himself a few more years. But then he would have missed his appointed rendezvous with Halley's Comet in 1910. He wouldn't have missed that for the world. "I came in with Halley's Comet in 1835," he said in 1909. "It's coming again next year, and I expect go out with it. It will be the greatest disappointment of my life if I don't go out with Halley's Comet. The Almighty has said, no doubt, 'Now here are these two unaccountable freaks; they came in together, they must go out together.' Oh! I am looking forward to that."

Whoever has lived long enough to find out what life is, knows how deep a debt of gratitude we owe to Adam, the first great benefactor of our race. He brought death into the world.

—*Pudd'nhead Wilson* (1894)

I think we never become really and genuinely our entire and honest selves until we are dead—and not then until we have been dead years and years. People ought to start dead, and they would be honest so much earlier.

—*Mark Twain in Eruption* (1940)

It is a pathetic thought. We struggle, we rise, we tower in the zenith a brief and gorgeous moment, with the adoring eyes of the nations upon us, then the lights go out, oblivion closes around us, our glory fades and vanishes, a few generations drift by, and naught remains but a mystery and a name.

—"The Secret History of Eddypus"

Pity is for the living, envy is for the dead.

—*Following the Equator* (1897)

All say, "How hard it is that we have to die"—a strange complaint to come from the mouths of people who have had to live.

—*Pudd'nhead Wilson* (1894)

Each person is born to one possession which outvalues all his others—his last breath.

—*Following the Equator* (1897)

The Impartial Friend: Death, the only immortal who treats us all alike, whose pity and whose peace and whose refuge are for all—the soiled and the pure, the rich and the poor, the loved and the unloved.

—last written statement, in
Moments With Mark Twain (Albert Bigelow Paine)

Palmists, clairvoyants, seers, and other kinds of fortune tellers all tell me that I am going to die, and I have the utmost admiration for their prediction. Perhaps they would convince me a little more of its truth if they told me the date.

—*The New York Times* (1907)

Death . . . a great Leveler—a king before whose tremendous majesty shades & differences in littleness cannot be discerned—an Alp from whose summit all small things are the same size.

—1871 letter

Both marriage and death ought to be welcome: the one promises happiness, doubtless the other assures it.

—1888 letter

I think this funeral is going to be a great thing. I shall be there . . . Shall I have a band? Land! I shall have fifty bands, falling over one another at every fifty yards, and each playing a different tune. It'll be a showy funeral, with plenty of liquor for the guests.

—*The New York Times* (1907)

Why there was a lady on board asked me to come to her wedding. "Yes," I replied. "I will if you'll come to my funeral." I told her all about it, and now she's quite eager for it to happen.

—*The New York Times* (1907)

As for me, I hope to be cremated. I made that remark to my pastor once, who said, with what he seemed to think was an impressive manner: "I wouldn't worry about that, if I had your chances."

—*Life on the Mississippi* (1883)

Epitaphs are cheap, and they do a poor chap a world of good after he is dead, especially if he had hard luck while he was alive. I wish they were used more.

—"A Curious Dream"

A distinguished man should be as particular about his last words as he is about his last breath. He should write them out on a slip of paper and take the judgment of his friends on them. He should never leave such a thing to the last hour of his life, and trust to an intellectual spurt at the last moment to enable him to say something smart with his latest gasp and launch into eternity with grandeur.

—"The Last Words of Great Men" (1869)

Heaven for climate, and hell for society.

—1901 speech

Travel has no longer any charm for me. I have seen all
the foreign countries I want to except heaven & hell
& I have only a vague curiosity about one of those.

—1891 letter

[Heaven and hell] I am silent on the subject because
of necessity. I have friends in both places.

—quoted in *Mark Twain, His Life and Work,*
by Will Clemens

When I reflect upon the number of disagreeable people
who I know have gone to a better world, I am moved
to lead a different life.

—*Pudd'nhead Wilson* (1894)

Miss Watson, a tolerable slim old maid, with goggles
on . . . told me all about the bad place, and I said I
wished I was there. She got mad then, but I didn't
mean no harm. All I wanted was to go somewheres; all
I wanted was a change, I warn't particular. She said it
was wicked to say what I said; said she wouldn't say it
for the whole world; she was going to live so as to go
to the good place. Well, I couldn't see no advantage

in going where she was going, so I made up my mind I wouldn't try for it. But I never said so, because it would only make trouble, and wouldn't do no good.

—*Adventures of Huckleberry Finn* (1885)

I have never seen what to me seemed an atom of proof that there is a future life. And yet—I am inclined to expect one.

—quoted in *Mark Twain: A Biography* (1912)
by Albert Bigelow Paine

Satan (impatiently) to New Comer. The trouble with you Chicago people is, that you think you are the best people down here; whereas you are merely the most numerous.

—*Following the Equator* (1897)

Heaven goes by favor. If it went by merit, you would stay out and your dog would go in.

—quoted in *Mark Twain: A Biography* (1912)
by Albert Bigelow Paine

ACKNOWLEDGMENTS

I'm going to start with Caroline Thomas Harnsberger, because she kind of started this whole business of extracting and arranging maxims, quotable lines, wit, and wisdom from Mark Twain's works. She arranged them in an encyclopedic A-to-Z manner in her landmark 1948 collection, *Mark Twain at Your Fingertips*. She was the godmother of this type of book. She also was a good friend to Twain's daughter, Clara. So we are in her debt for taking the early lead in this field and showing the way.

The modern potentates in the realm of Mark Twain quotability are two incredibly generous scholars, Barbara Schmidt and R. Kent Rasmussen. Barb runs twainquotes.com, and Kent is the editor of the most reliable collection of Twain quotes, *The Quotable Mark Twain: His Essential Aphorisms, Witticisms & Concise Opinions* (1997). I am grateful to both of them for not only their expertise and guidance but for years of friendship. I started building this concept about twenty years ago. I met Barb and Kent a few years later, and, since then, I haven't made a move in Twain territory without consulting them.

Indeed, the works of countless incredibly giving scholars have increased my enthusiasm for Mark Twain and deepened my understanding of him. It has been one of the honors of my life to count so many of them as friends. And that list begins with Hal Holbrook, whose *Mark Twain Tonight!* first lured me under the spell of the writer's words. The quotes in this book have been culled from Twain's novels, travel books, short stories, essays, letters, speeches, journalism, interviews, and autobiographical writings, yet the influence of each of these fellow Twainiacs has been profound.

I'd also like to recognize the belief and support (and tenacity) of my agent, Charlotte Gusay. Mark Twain said there was "no surer way to find out whether you like people or hate them than to travel with them." Charlotte has been great good company as we've traveled this road with Mr. Twain.

Equally good company has been Colleen Dunn Bates, who gave this book a wonderful home at Prospect Park Books. She has brought new meaning to a Twain line in this collection: "Work and play are words used to describe the same thing under different conditions." The work, if you want to call it that, has been incalculable fun.

And my greatest debt of gratitude, as ever, is to Sara and Becky, who share the laughter and the love, at each turn of the road.

ABOUT THE AUTHOR

MARK DAWIDZIAK is the television critic for the *Cleveland Plain Dealer*. A theater, film, and television reviewer for more than thirty years, he has written several books, including *Mark My Words: Mark Twain on Writing* (St. Martin's Press) and *Horton Foote's The Shape of the River: The Lost Teleplay About Mark Twain* (Applause). In addition to his work as a Twain scholar, Dawidziak has been playing Twain on stage for more than thirty years. His other books include the horror novel *Grave Secrets*, *The Bedside, Bathtub & Armchair Companion to Dracula*, the literary biography *Jim Tully: American Writer, Irish Rover, Hollywood Brawler* (with Paul J. Bauer), and two histories of landmark TV series: *The Columbo Phile: A Casebook* and *The Night Stalker Companion*. Dawidziak and his wife, actress Sara Showman, founded the Largely Literary Theater Company in 2002 to promote literacy, literature, and live theater. They live in Cuyahoga Falls, Ohio, with their daughter, Rebecca "Becky" Claire.